I0155922

LOVE

poems by Gordon Massman

NQY Books™

The New York Quarterly Foundation, Inc.
New York, New York

NYQ Books™ is an imprint of The New York Quarterly Foundation, Inc.

The New York Quarterly Foundation, Inc.
P. O. Box 2015
Old Chelsea Station
New York, NY 10113

www.nyq.org

Copyright © 2014 by Gordon Massman

All rights reserved. No part of this book may be used or reproduced in any manner whatsoever without written permission of the author except in the case of brief quotations embodied in critical articles and reviews.

First Edition

Layout and Design by Jessica S. Eichman | www.glasseggdesign.com
Cover Design by Noah Saterstrom | www.noahsaterstrom.com

Library of Congress Control Number: 2014933704

ISBN: 978-1-935520-96-2
ISBN for set: 978-1-935520-98-6

for Patricia Corley

and in memory of my parents Edward and Roslyne Massman

Sometimes I think if we have *chosen* to love someone,
we love them even more than we do the children of our bodies.

—Eleanor Roosevelt

PART I

My mistress' eyes…

*M*Y WIFE'S mouth and teeth remind me of mouth and teeth of
hyena, javelina, hammerhead, rat, porcupine, bat, aardvark,
also beetle, mantis, and water-bug mandible; reminiscent
of chimpanzee, snapping turtle, wildebeest, steenbok,
skunk, pigeon, frog is her neck; hands and arms echo
starfish, Rottweiler, sea urchin, meerkat, grizzly, octopus,
brown recluse; breasts recall images of hog, opossum,
humpback whale, Bactrian camel, elephant, titmouse,
sloth—teats, mammaries, nipples, heft; hair mimics
hair of loris, tamarind, mountain beaver, tarantula,
bird of paradise, blow fly, dik-dik, armadillo, protecting,
warming, terrifying, attracting; her hips, curvaceous
hemispheres, dune-smooth slopes have no truck with
donkey-baboon-capybara-woodchuck-kangaroo hips
and the ponderously pounding buttocked hippopotamus
odiferously trouncing mangroves of muck and crushed
nannyberry pungent as paradise-ground finger root,
fennel, caraway, and wattle seed in nature's natural
mortar and pestle bowl; oh, her genitals one wants
to compare with apricot, mango, fig, red plum but
these mindless rotters pale beside genitalia of the
buffalo, duiker, polecat, wild ass, pronghorn, tapir, and
common mongrel, prominent, glorious, folded, pulchri-
tudinous; her ass—incomparable—but let's whirl,
scorpion, black fly, walking stick, mud dauber, red ant,
Canada goose, greater flamingo, manta ray, Sumatran
rhinoceros, emperor penguin; my love's taut vein-
wrapped ankles, who but I dare analogize, blue-footed
booby, nanny goat, pileated woodpecker, reticulated
giraffe, Komodo dragon, hundred-booted centipede,
funnel weaver, American quarter horse, toad, cricket, tick,
and the circumducta satyr, irresistible, erotic, narco-
tizing; and I being sucker of toes, toe connoisseur

polished or nude, dominant middle, excruciatingly
stepped, stubby or slender must only mention thick
black wedges of mud squeezed upward between
downward plunging over-burdened Russian yak, suck
and squish, clots tearing off and splatting, wedge rising
between toes, scraping hooves, folding back into
sludge slowly, torpidly, a languid slop as she plods
in putty river; finally, that cumulative coordination
of the entire: her carriage, my love's compilation of
prehistoric bones floating in muscle, anchored in grace,
with the core-centered balance of ballerina, my
love's spine, clavicle, shoulders, toes, supple but
erect, thumbs forward, unparalleled yogi-master
quality equipoise of the traverse and sagittal plane
not unlike streptococci, bacilli, paramecium, amoeba,
nucleotide, sea jelly, wooly caterpillar, backward
popping prawn, vole, lemming, duck-billed platypus;
all these she, plus Galapagos tortoise, great frigate
bird; she lumbers in beauty like polar bear, rump
ascendant, snout downward, coat of white needles,
udders jolting, slashing blubber, cracking skulls,
rearing occasionally on massive thighs to frosted
crimson berries, spearing at icy table with God-
sculpted claws flesh, organs, feathers, and sauces.

I **LOVE** you like a Kraft caramel, like a paper kite, like a blue-green chameleon,
I love you like the yellow Texas rose, like bluebonnet, the black-eyed Susan,
I love you like the Plaza, the Barbizon, the Algonquin, the Azure Banyon Tree,
I love you like chocolate mousse, like Passover gelt, like the Corvette Sting Ray,
I love you like books, like sharp pencils, like wooden toothpicks in May,
I love you like Band-Aids, like animal crackers, like the Anti-Defamation
        League,
I love you like psychoanalysis, like Double Stuff, like Charmin Ultra Soft,
I love you like rock candy mountain, like gastroenterological regularity, like the
        absence of TV,
I love you like rolled up sleeves, like blister-less toes, like other people's
        failures,
I love you like Michigan J. Frog, like necessary brain surgery, like un-nicked
        tweezers,
I love you like Crayola brand Razzamatazz tangerine crayon,
I love you like Desenex, like Victorinox, like Vladimir Nabokov,
I love you like men who break women's hearts and fix them for repeat
        performance,
I love you like Ibuprofen, like Carl Theodore Dryer, like 3-in-1 oil,
I love you like general anesthesia, like dead parents, like the absence of pets,
I love you like MiraLAX, like Elmer's glue, like Robinson Jeffers,
I love you like antidisestablishmentarianism, usufruct, like uxorious,
I love you like the Bugatti Veyron, like Vacheron Constantin, like potato peeler,
I love you like fraudulent religious artifacts, defrocked convicted pederasts, and
        dead fascists,
I love you like Deet in Spring, like raspberry bread pudding, like suicide before
        murder,
I love you like rabbits, like Winchester 30-30s, like leather bull whips,
I love you like children confiscated from abusive parents, like a fresh sketchpad,
        like weight loss,
I love you like Divorce Court, like Wild Bill Hickok, like celebrity cellulite,
I love you like under-tipping, like getting something for nothing, like removed
        road kill,

I love you like adulterous politicians, desecrated crucifixes, Eyjafjallajokull's
eruption,

I love you like new car smell, vine ripe tomato, picking toenails in bed while
watching Jean-Paul Belmondo blow off his painted blue head
with dynamite belt,

I love you like Huckleberry Hound, like Mercurochrome, like huntsman's
aluminum shaft spinning towards roebuck's heart,

I love you like shaving cream, like atheists, like the ecstasy of championship
over devastated competitors,

I love you like baby photos, childhood photos, yearbook portraits, like fatal
vehicular accidents in which life goes on, like photos of
grandchildren,

I love you like anti-Semitic gore caked on a car fender, like the amaryllis, like
Hellman's Real Mayonnaise prior to ptomaine poisoning,

I love you like retsina, like liquid nails, like King Kong,

I love you like I love the moment sissy surpasses bully in dominance and
solidity, bully a mushy quasi-alcoholic fat-boy facing impotence
and beautiful mirages, I love you more than I savor his eventual
suicide,

I love you like Pez dispensers, like Comet cleanser, like the apprehension and
execution of escaped Nazi collaborators ensconced in Argentina
or Czechoslovakia with wives and butchered meat and antibiotic
pills,

I love you like Nicanor Parra, like shore bird squawk, like intrepid explorer in
deepest reaches growing beard of worms and mosquitoes,

I love you like dead radios, like laryngitis, like the paradise between symphony
orchestras,

I love you like Aunt Jemima, Log Cabin, Canadian maple syrup, cane sugar, beet
sugar, black strap, Karo, agave, brown rice syrup, barley malt,
date sugar, honey, apple syrup, turbinado sugar, sugar in the raw,
and spreadable fruit, like Tootsie Roll Pops, like cocaine, like
dissolution, obesity, bulimia, body dsymorphic disorder, circus
mirrors, binge eaters, and one trick ponies,

I love you like surfboards, like Briggs & Stratton two stroke engine, like The
　　　　　Beach Boys' *God Only Knows* and *Caroline No*, like a boy's
　　　　　first kiss, like the poignant exuberant hair-covered crushability
　　　　　of the back of a young man's head, like summer swelter
　　　　　drowned yellow jacket summer swimming pool Creamsicle with
　　　　　half-naked mother towel-tanning on scorched green poolside
　　　　　grass with friends, like penny flickering through water to
　　　　　deep end drain and scissor-legging through thudding emerald
　　　　　explosions,
I love you like trap set Troggs and Yardbirds amateur banging in shut-door
　　　　　bedroom, *Heart Full of Soul, Wild Thing* megalomaniacal,
　　　　　euphoric, and immortally-pumping, like larvae, pupa, cocoon,
　　　　　butterfly, like the pushing, teeming, swollen insect and maggot
　　　　　rivers and oceans riddling, beneath its skin, Earth's corpulent
　　　　　body, collectively the blood of the planet,
I love you like individuality, like peppermint toothpaste, like shutting to
　　　　　external influences earlids severing to silence repercussion
　　　　　and reprimand such as ostracism, marginalization, expulsion
　　　　　from the power-herd and mother dust cloud choking sun and
　　　　　asphyxiating lungs with powder,
I love you like ducks, like bandanas, like bananas,
I love you like Disneyland version of Davy Crockett, men of leather, sweat, and
　　　　　integrity, fight-to-death blunderbuss men, but non-threatening
　　　　　sensitive husbands, survival-adept, self-educated, half cougar,
　　　　　half tortoise wielding axe and delivering calf, and hefting and
　　　　　hurling boulders into creek, who thrust forged steel into boiling
　　　　　heart and butchers the meat, and die altruistically in a distant
　　　　　fort,
I love you like ducks, like islands, like yo-yo tricks,
I love you like continuous low-level depression-narcissism's near-perfect
　　　　　manipulation of intimates, swinging attention to my catastrophe
　　　　　and spidering outward the illusion of seductive torment, half
　　　　　an ingrained deliberate tactic to win female sympathy, half

justifiable melancholy of the hypersensitive personality, like
electric staplers, like parrots,

I love you like Balinese children, like Chinese children, like Ethiopian children,
oh hell, like all brassy fascinated audacious overconfident
dictatorial voracious children-optimists, like Mississippian grits,
like Wilson Staff golf balls,

I love you like Renee Maria Falconetti, like Anna Karina, like black-faced
Monica Vitti in a Roman condominium African drum-dancing
with spear, like a pocket full of pine cones,

I love you like disgust, like vulgarity, like Babinski reflex, like brutal truth, like
sour cherries, like despising the despicable and, Christianity be
damned, wishing them malfunction, maladjustment, malnutrition,
malpractice, and malaria,

I love you like The Palladium 1977, Frank Zappa, *Black Napkins,* like 1966,
Fresh Cream, *I'm So Glad,* like Bethel, NY, August 17, 1969, *I'm
Going Home,* Ten Years After, like rural nighttime darkness, like
rage,

I love you like rage, like bitterness, like onomatopoeia, like animadversion,
like laziness, like in late night Roman alleyways white-fox-
coated Anita Ekberg balancing a Persian kitten on head prior
to smashing with lust Marcello Mastroianni's obsequious and
foolish face,

I love you like a psychologically stable, sexually questionable male fashion
model trekking the Himalayas in L.L. Bean Pathfinder Cargo
Pants, Moose River Hat, and Vintage Field Watch, interrupting a
twenty-three thousand foot ascent for banana and Cliff Bar under
cloudless skies in mid-afternoon surrounded by delphiniums, like
cattle torsos on hooks stringing blood in slaughter houses, like
Plato, like Worcestershire sauce,

I love you like terrified patients in ambulances who are not me splitting
traffic *en route* to intubations, neuromuscular blockades,
pneumonectomies, skin grafts, amputations, like sharp scissors,
like Hershey Kisses, like son's plexus absorbing father's

knuckles,

I love you like the infinite hallways of me posing between two mirrors, like
                gasoline odors, like cordoned crime scenes, like pickle relish,
                natural catastrophes including fires, power outages, flooding,
                emergency shelters, and devastated families,

I love you like Carnation Condensed Milk, like bicarbonate of soda, like a
                perfect score,

I love you like tearful catharsis, like the shamed humiliated season-losing goalie
                slumping to locker room paper-cup pelted dragging headgear
                like a broken spine, like Calamine lotion, like tin sheriff badge,
                like stadium of devastation and false sportsmanship littered with
                wet confetti and nacho mangers, like flat-on-back marital and
                financial failure prior to resurrection as a jackknife or furious
                humanist,

I love you like the meanest, whitest white-supremacist son-of-a-bitch in creation
                with his brickbat, credo, and magnanimous wife assassinated
                at cookout by Emmitt Till, Medgar Evers, Malcolm X, Louis
                Farrakhan, W.E.B. Dubois, like cat's eye marbles, like Komodo
                dragon,

I love you like glitter, like buckskin Cody coat with rattlesnake vertebrae beads,
                like Robitussin,

I love you like the apocalypse, like asunder, black sun, monstrous scorpion,
                nihilism, implacable vengeance, social breakdown, decadence,
                bestiality, like priests in tutus, like gapped front teeth, like
                Chevy's 1967 Nova Super Sport L-79, 12.5 quarter mile, like
                Maalox, like Dan Blocker, George Maharis, and Richard Boone
                turned-up black leather collar facing the cold,

I love you like sleeves and strong hands bridged by muscle, integument, tendon,
                clamping dense awkward objects like human beings, furniture,
                tree stumps, yoke and plow, scarred, nicked, torn, calloused,
                broad, or rocking dejected head like an ostrich egg, like
                seaweed, like Andre Schwarz-Bart, like the conflicted brain,

I love you like physical object the saxophone, complicated exoskeleton of

rods, pins, neck, bell, lids, like the rail job's welded fleshless
bones connected to pure radical performance or nothing but
architectural stand-still, both capable with the human soul
of extreme power, speed and will, like Spanish Brush, like
hummingbird feeder, like a wind-whipped, weather-shredded,
viscerally-torn northern Maine island American flag sagging on
a white pole, like dead emblems and curled parchment scrawled
with ancient prayer and lamentation,

I love you like Saguaro cactus, like *Coup de Torchon's* Cordier executing with
pistol two insignificant hectoring ruffians after a total eclipse
of the sun, like surgically inserted aluminum knee pins, like the
osprey, like the terminally ill mentally ripping off bedclothes
when in reality merely ineffectually clutching at rags to die as
they were born, naked,

I love you like old Bijous, like Tabasco sauce, like creel of regrets,

I love you like full metal jacket .350 magnum from mid-distance spraying
Hitler's Final Solution out back of his head, like Comrade
Napoleon, like collision of passions in wounded woman facing
once again gorgeous abuser, like Mr. Pibb, like laser beams
exploding the kidney stone,

I love you like Happiness's beast effortlessly sliding off his drowned wife onto
his mistress, like poisonous wasps and heavy nectar-dirigibles
droning to master hive, like two friend-enemies on opposite sides
of scrimmage after snapped ball pushing each other so ruthlessly
what's between squeezes up in curled sheets like cheese,

I love you like delirium tremens, like Coco Puffs, like what stone man
becomes—blood heart and bowels—when experience over-opens
him to empathy compassion tenderness love—an automatic
governor against petrification, dead robotic eyes staring through
and into distances, split from himself and survival, like Opie
Taylor, like Sweeney Todd, eyes like ashen coals, like Boris and
Natasha,

I love you like lawn mowers against nature's surge, trees dropping cones,

swelling, muscling in, the battle clash at yard's perimeter
between pine, oak, maple, ash, monkey grass, only asphalt
triumphs over sapling, paved moats surrounding Albany, Des
Moines, Indianapolis—freeway loops, strip malls, parking
lots—and still Ursa Major defecates Amazons onto sprinkler
system, like oatmeal, like Neosporin,
I love you like pink lemonade, like cupolas, like weather vanes,
I love you like noiselessness, like stick candy, like the Butcher of Buchenwald's
toothache,
I love you like the red giant, black hole, white dwarf, supernova, Andromeda,
event horizon cosmic psychedelic insanity—psilocybin,
mescaline, lysergic acid—twirling through mind alternately
megalomaniacal phantasmagoria and suicidal insignificance,
frothing wordlessness, like the ceaseless washing machine
overloaded with soap, like nonpareils, like Arabian knives,
I love you like Freddie the Freeloader, like Sam I Am, like war casualties
encased in lime Jell-O slurped by God and His Seven Angels,
Shadi, Nuoko, Kelja, Shianka, Savi, Toomdja, and Nkaawadj,
ladies all, spooning piquant skulls, fruity thighs, scrotum,
colon, eyes from chilled metallic bowls dripping sweat and
mayonnaise from sky mansions,
I love you like castrati, like Benito Mussolini, like cat scratch fever and its
ghost hallucinations of Imelda Marcos, Baudelaire, and Harry
Houdini escaping with a delphinium and bromeliad bouquet
from a clamped and locked Iron Maiden inside a solid concrete
block,
I love you like *in absentia,* like Erick Von Zipper, like night dreams with
oceans, always oceans sucking, rip-tiding, tugging ankles,
sweeping sea-foam across itself, and I hauling in crappie or red
snapper, mackintosh, wading boots, rubber storm hat fluttering
like ragged paper against a raging infinity point, foliage-
woven surf—roots, runners, branches, vines, leaves, needles,
blossoms—whole liquid jungles lifting and dropping cargoes

through muscled self, and I surf-riding past high-rises, sea walls,
spectators with pets, buttresses and embankments against the
raging rhyme,

I love you like this and this and this and fingers and crab legs and tool boxes
and light houses and picture frames and pot holders and Milton
Bradley and assassinations and hippopotamuses and river silt
and transformer boxes and dog whiskers and mortality and
Ingmar Bergman and Henkel cutlery and Peter Pan dust and the
Transfiguration and Eagle Claw hooks and reptile assassination
and Black Cat explosions and motor boats and gypsum and
spinning tin carousels and Kensington beach shirts and the
Russian steppes and Sergei Eisenstein and baby caterwaul and
Betty Boop and cardiac surgery and blueberry cobbler and
spousal abuse and influenza and Finnan Haddie and slug juice
and whorling grottoes and rail splitter nails and reinforced walls
and Alex DeLarge and Log Cabin Syrup and failed mathematics
and antique hat pins and deceased Llaso Apsos and Morton
Thiakol and the holy communion plate and intergalactic travel
and profligate bankruptcy and suicide by hanging and stainless
Moen fixtures and the Mariana Trench and Quetzalcoatl and fly
bonfires and bleached clavicles and double hung windows and
myoepithelial carcinoma and sickle cell anemia and clear thread
noodles and Chief Halfoat and high-powered deer rifles and clog
dancing and bloody knuckles and motorized remote airplanes
and Halvah and Black Gulch Rock and cigarillos & and & and
& and the man shot from cannon who catches trapeze mid-air
back flips lands on platform dives into bucket half-full of water
springboards to feet and squirts jet from lapel daisy to standing
ovation of cousins and children and sodden fathers and milk
shook mothers and uncles flipping nickels for nephew and niece
and gesticulating ridiculously like clowns,

Like all the aforesaid standing on Earth's surface and all that lies under in bands
and striations in rock and ice and fire and glacier unexpressed,

unperceived, or, as yet, undiscovered I love you and love you and love you.

*G*OAT FECES, locust blood, tortoise urine infest Jesus's toe nails, that staff-wielding idiot in love and lust with his lunatic fleece-flock and dangling circumcision, Mary grinding wash over rock, cocks and robes, I mean God damn, nutcase central, eyelash dust, poverty, vultures, mud cakes, scorpion stinging sand creatures, side-winder snakes, holy shit! and this filthy-footed megalomaniac spouting euphemisms at the starving, big stir, neon nipples, everyone tenderized and horrified by death into superstition, our Boy an opportunist charismatic hawking hut-to-hut a sort of biblical World Book and inspiring mass hysteria, what the hell, defying physical law and the hot smite of entropy, Jeptha, Abidah, and Zadoc trading ploughshares for hallucinations, fear makes lovers of us all, I love God through fear of meaninglessness, sterility, extinction, impoverishment brushed off like sand stuck to flesh, I devoted unswerving supplicant, let us pray, I am unafraid, shadow and valley, hurricane, muddy bottom, Jesus's finger-nails grimy with chaff, goat oil, vagina juice, King of Jews, and I among the soldiers, chewing Double Bubble, who nailed Him up, echoing hammer-blows of warped devotion, smoke rising, women wailing, the whole megillah, fornicators, pretzel ven-dors, glo-whips, braid of blood, and I forty generations later still a human love machine muffled, throbbing, soft, satiated.

*W*HIPLASH BINDS Fenwick to railroad track, ground rumbles, train, shuddering, approaches, collapses time, Whiplash twists mustachios, Fenwick wriggles, shrieks, secretly oozes something wonderful, Whiplash, humpbacked, squash-headed, fiendishly rubs hands, bulges pants, draping rails Fenwick's thick strawberry locks, apron thigh-hiked, wide brassiere, puff-clouds stack like dishes, shrill-like Kestrel, sinister giggles, from nowhere suddenly appears riding backward on Horse Do-Right, prominent jaw, uniform, creased white hat, dismounts in dust wisp, unties ten-handed death-knot, Do-Right! Nell shouts, don't you fucking get it, moron! idiot! sex-game, sado-masochism, I permit it, exciting, exhilarating, erotic, always snatches me fibrillating last-millimeter, hauls to mill, fucks me silly, but you miscalculating blockhead invariably intervene, ruin, stick to headquarters stupid Mountie in your boredom chair, I crave precipice, danger, deviance, sure, I look virginal but beware perfect packages, he beats me and I like it, I fume but crave his whips, while bled white baby-veal you in this Canadian hellhole embody squeamish con-siderateness, lip balm, Milquetoast conformity, Home Sweet Home Whitman sampler, good god in house slippers I rot of tedium, thong panties underneath granny gown Nell lashed to log churns toward ripsaw, screams, God O God! save! rescue! Whiplash salivates, again bulges, Nell from ecstasy-crease slippery-secretes, saw rages, blade smokes, voltage surges, sequestered mill filled with burnt log pieces, chains, pulp hooks, swinging tongs, winch straps, wood chipper, legs spread tight, disk bears down on Fenwick's gash, pressure, sweat, erect nipples, fantastic oblivion, Nell's brain malfunctions, sheer hormones, Snidley, crazed, envisions desperation-sex, locked and panting, snail-trail spit across naked shoulder, tanned hard pectoral, seldom seen his ripped physique, just before blade vivisects poor baby Dudley outleaps sex-primed Snidely by a split, scoops her onto Horse, god dammed disgustingly faithful wrong-headed lunatic interjecting erroneous assumption always and once again, cuffing Snidely after roughing him up, oh Nell, Darling Princess, Precious One, yes, and his mesmerizing underappreciated horse Horse, Jesus fuck! she screams, I just want some whisky and a good old fashioned masochistic strapping, Dudley, Dudley, oh Dudley, get out my life.

*L*IFE I WANT, the gutsy brawling footballer bearded big-handed
shoved around mug gut-laughing bust-in-chops life, not this
squeamish neurotic soft-fingered over-analyzed liberal-
multicultural nonviolent literature-obsessed idiocy, the
Jim Bowie Davy Crockett kind of thing with knife, black
powder and hands thrust in animal guts bleeding out gun
wound goddammit, not this Salade Nicoise, lyonnaise squirt-
squiggled over pear braised pullet candied pecan crap
which is why I married you and your Glock Harley Doberman
Pincer bookless torture chamber chains electrical
tools saw blades whirling through steel tables propane,
pressure pump and gauges smeared-stained-scraped-
cracked concrete floor, you taught me kill zone, circulatory
system epicenter instantaneously bringing down
Bambi, Hop Thief, Southwark Premium, King Cobra
Malt, daredevil sex, The de Havilland Twin Otter skid,
bite and back-flesh rake on elephant grass sub-Sahara
nails-in-sky god nakedness, pulled me from snail shell
with demitasse fork all curled brown like a miniature
coward, goose pimple-nipple male and taught me
glacial lichen-bearded howling ice and Aurora Borealis
grit in cultivated Boston, ice blossoms tightening glass
and caveman clog dancing, which is why you for this
salamander lily pond serenity gardener with his gross-
beak waxwing cowbird black sunflower seed binocular,
thank god Tyrannosaurus rex Piscataway-hatched
you on a Big Daddy Roth cream machine goggled
eating raw gar, life I wanted and ditched the fob and
hair-clippers and frozen cod and Numb-Zit gel, and
hiked up britches for the ribcage-ripping lifelong throb.

I KNEW I LOVED when you revealed that you took into home and
nursed for years your terminally ill former husband, cleaning
shit, lifting off rug, diapering, wiping drool, barring door
from neighborhood wandering, sacrificing fulfillment until,
hand clasping yours, he died in Albuquerque, I knew I
loved when despite filmmaking's transparent contrivances—
camera, costume, lighting, script—you shielded eyes from
watching in his phantasmagoric film, *The Mirror,* Tarkovsky's
peasant behead her chicken, I knew I loved when among
five domestic animals—Ginger, Tulip, Rosie, Sydney,
Mittens—you resented none, spread over each your physical
blanket of inexhaustible warmth, I knew I loved when you
sped past King of Prussia Mall en route to Goodwill to
procure wardrobe and Waterford, I knew I loved when
from merely conjuring past distress you squeezed sour
lemon juice tears off facial precipice where injustice and
humiliation pool, I knew I loved when you appeared one
foot socked in big pink lips, the other in ski-capped
penguins, I knew I loved when you spilled from backpack
beach glass pieces and, precious as eggs, ocean-tumbled
stones inlaid with rings, your marvelous trove disgorged
gratis by sea's lodestar treasure-heave, I knew I loved
when you raged, then, heartbroken, collapsed after the
new efficiency-principal accused you of treason for de-
fending rights of special needs kids: Jessyka's Asperger's,
Marley's ADD, Zach's oppositional defiance disorder, col-
lectively the object of your uncompromising passionate
expertise for whose equality you would, I am positive,
die, I knew I loved when you married to trunk onto health
insurance plan a man with myoepithelial carcinoma of
the parotid gland, he being I who received the parotid-
ectomy and radiotherapy at zero personal expense
defrauding the industry, five years later in Plainfield,
Massachusetts we remain devoted, solvent, and satisfied.

*M*ISOGYNISTS AND man-haters make the greatest lovers,
sex maniacs hammering partners in sticky sweat, ripped,
grooved, defined, rock-hard iron-pumpers, sweat band,
lipstick, glittery laces, sharp cruel faces, after narcissistic
seduction wrathfully coupling in swank apartments
secretly loathing each other, genitals blunt instruments,
Dick despising mother vivisects lover with objectification,
tight cunt, etc., while Prissy sucking cock fantasizes
secreting acid, goddamn rapacious controlling bastards
plowing flesh with serrated edges, making deals by
cellphone, each compulsively wishes to exterminate
the opposite gender which is why male-bashers and
misogynists make the best lovers, precision, position,
technique, timing working bodies like Snap-on
tools, the just-right fitting and grip, brilliant accuracy,
ball bearings floating in sealed encasement, master-
ful performance including the invidious climactic
blather, man-haters beyond reproach with silicon
tits, and irresistible misogynists with fascinating
collections: immaculate complete sets in velvet-lined
boxes, engraved, authenticated, or meticulously
pinned under glass display case, superior, lethal,
perfectionistic and sleek, deceptively gentle demeanor
and empathetic expression, I remember particulars
of my fabulous fascism, savoring domination with
military exactness, my penis a shiv thrust into
mother, stabbing and stabbing, her orgasmic squeal
a capitulation, and they sectioning me like butcher's
meat-map, tenderloin, rib eye, New York Strip which
with whetted blades they devoured like father, that
incalculable monster, spittle and fist, unable to love
women, before my heart burst like an overfilled
bladder, and the incomprehensible metamorphosis.

*H*OW DARE you have the nerve to love me or try to control
the velocity of my love, I do not acquiesce, I am narcissist,
not philanthropist, nobody possesses this, I expunge
while kissing, nothing is absolute, love too is blemished
with conflict, stroking you is dissonance, revulsion of
happiness, behind radiance lies rival self-destruction,
behind voluptuousness desiccation, I who adore you—
blown glass, monarch wing—cannot tolerate the nerve-
tangle of extreme colonization, there is, however, this:
slender discus whirling off thrower's fingertips, grunting
catharsis, momentary freedom of lift, back sweat, pit-
trickle, bulging muscle, his monolithic roar, yes, males
love bluntly, gill-blood, gutted roe, raw and red, males
love like backhoe blade in arterial flood, (women,
never mind), men lock in fiery glare sumptuous morsel,
men such as I resent ownership, enter mothers,
possessive, vengeful, shower-streaming nipples, let
us not repress men's formidable ruthless terror of
impotence coiled in the brain lobe like polio, dare
you, I repeat, clap my heart in your buttermilk, your
viscous nog, goddamn you, this blustery narcissist, this
single-headed mob, tongue by tongue violent of self-
interest, shielded, encrusted, blunting all comers, yet
I keep thinking of discus thrower, iron stiff, spring-
loaded, absolute focus, spinning, spinning, releasing.

I SHARE MOVIES with you, *Coup de Torchon, Au Husard Balthazar, La Belle et la Bete,* what I love I require you to love, we prop heads against pillows, I press play, faces flare, *La Bete Humaine* in which an obsessive-compulsive male murders women he adores, imperative that you respect this work or you dis-respect me, at random intervals, wide-eyed, glancing askance, I interrogate, "like it?" "awake?" I stake pride, my critical acumen and pressure you, pretending liberality apply in-security's tourniquet, twisting the knot, I cannot tolerate your disapprobation—imagined or otherwise—threaten to kill the film, wounded and compelled Jean Gabin's tormented protagonist repulses you as does the dominant motif of psychopathic misogyny, tortured infantile men incapable of tenderness perpetrating simplistic violence in the guise of complexity, irking me the movie disgusts you, I pretend indifference, exonerate, acknowledge law of multiplicity of palates while hardening round my rock of endeavor, repudiation, embracing, naturally, differences in taste yet insisting that certain world master-pieces have achieved by consensus universal appeal, Michelangelo's Pieta, Beethoven's 5th, surely Renoir's brilliant orchestration deserves absolute acclamation, but, more fundamentally I cannot bear my failure to bring home treasure displeasing you, and deflate in my craving for universal heroism, as my father—indisput-able buffoon—failed his princess earning her undying extirpation, turning to you my backside in bed, tightly I clamp round the intolerable sting of primal inadequacy.

*T*ODAY MY death day, "I love you," heart feels, but body cannot
speak it, indecipherable blather, dementia misshapes me,
gibberish, "honey bunch," "sweetie pie," "angel," but cannot
work lips, tongue a lead blanket, death day rhapsody, look
at these feet, what happened, numb, God splits us like cord-
wood, we're tragic, pathetic, me swollen, breathless, 71 over
40, you beautiful wild iris, don't go, stay beside my motorized
contraption, nothing when you go though still internally I
sing, oh baby, each breath my crematoria, locked in paralysis,
sublingual morphine, and Benadryl pudding, dissolving like
mist but love you with my scarlet lozenge, "baby love," I
try, nothing but stringy spittle, eyelash crust, mouth grit,
pooled wattles, gray dusty pate, touch me as I pass through
death's wobbly mirror that my last sensation will be fingers
sliding off, yours mine, mine yours, that ribbon-thin instant
between breath and extinction where love is held deepest.

*H*ETEROSEXUAL MEN want to penetrate pretty women, stick themselves in them, plant themselves, colonize, want to ruin them, too, for rivals, igniting incomparable euphoria, enslaving to their superior member, member that feels to pretty women like ten thick battering feet of muscular voltage, lipstick, toenail lacquer, mascara, heels, silk under- clothes, submission, infantilism ignite men, not cackle or pushiness, they want women who love to feel like hostages against razorblade, tied, vulnerable, punished like naughty Catholics inside network of belts and bedposts, legs plied, heterosexual men love cruelty and mock-cruelty and frustrated women whom when unleashed flood with voraciousness, devour their mates like ravenous vixens, mothers urinating, replacing maxipad, parading, posing nude before them addict sons to rage and satyriasis, who with unacknowledged misogyny compensate with heroin of erectile tissue, this written Valentine's Day, 2011, 3:38 PM, card to whom I love, goathead of sweet- ness wedged in urethra or basal lobe blocks certain hetero- sexual men sending them full of sludge or crud to psyche ward from which they emerge cranium sawn and stapled like plywood boxes, all night, quietly, these ones whimper.

*B*LOOD SCRIBBLING off His thorns, throbbing from His wrists, weeping down His wound, clotting in His feet, and a woman at the cross sucking him off.

*Y*OU LOVE ME because I am tortured, compulsive, conflicted, beautiful,
you love me because I am misanthropic, sardonic, negative, funny,
you love me because I am executioner, crucifier, mediator, clown,
you love me because I am Davy Crockett, Clark Kent, Cheyenne, Gore Vidal,
you love me because I am scurrilous, uninhibited, independent, contemptuous,
you love me because upon occasional gloomy impacted morning at bed's
    freezing periphery in Red Sox PJs spontaneously, like yesteryear-
    Dad pumping pouty girl's irrepressible giggle, I dance a jig in the
    ridiculous breakdown cacophony of Bozo Clown, Steve Martin,
    Jackie Gleason, Pinkie Lee,
you love me because sub-verbally, preternaturally, epileptically your genes,
    wildly twittering, pedal-to-metal, flutes wide open, identify in my
    genes—madly, apoplectically—biology's compatible evolutionary
    continuity,
you love me because femininity tinges my penis while masculinity shades my
    heart,
you love me because I am butch-wax, polo-shirt, school-supply, set-up, 1950s,
    red Huffy, Ruff, Ready, Heckle, Jeckle, Moe, Curly, Larry,
    Jackie Cooper, steak, atomic fission, pre-semen Mentholatum-
    obsessed, merit badge sash, major's pitcher, grape snow cone,
    Double Bubble, Black Cat, pirate's map of hidden vagina, British
    Sterling, Canoe, Tad racket, India Madras, 409, What Went Wrong,
    Wendy? Mickey's Big Mouth, Schlitz Malt Liquor, Hamm's Blue
    Water, unconsciously suicidal, formative alcoholic, enraged lizard
    murderer,
you love me because I am calamitous, impatient, impetuous, and fail
    spectacularly,
you love me because I have a thick dick,
you love me because all witnesses expired making me god's historiographer,
you love me because I fucked uxorious, animadversion, crepuscular, usufruct,
you love me because hours after disappearing behind a wall I reappear with ink-
    coated tongue and cavernous maw through which monkeys, bats,
    crows, and ants flow like a black alphabet,

you love me because I am a caramel-covered, marshmallow-blended, chocolate-
swirled, poppycock-blanketed, nervosa-anorectic, body-obsessed
hyper-neurotic, psychopathological, terror-of-extinction sugar
mainliner, dashing like a mouse cloak of night cake-to-sundae-
to-nausea-to-soft batch, each blast a corner into which boredom
shoved me, eschewed,

you love me because simultaneously I dumped from a lurching pick-up truck six
drums of paint dragging a rainbow across God's parking lot,

you love me because drunk on moonshine Fate bolted shut my skull after
shoving in brain's two halves, both apoplectically right,

you love me because thirteen years ago I slid under eye behind forehead bone
and rocked back-forth gleaming new putty knife slitting my TV's
frontal lobe, then jammed into its cyclopic eye dough-kneading
hook switched on high creating lobotomy of circuitry, plastic,
glass, malfunctioning holographs, because I blot with thumb
cold Coca-Cola sun and the innumerable impoverishing bodies
of dialectical materialism, with finger or hand obliterate entire
egotistical galaxies, because I disfigure with scissors and felt-tip
Izod, Polo, Converse, and God,

you love me because I French kissed Freud, buggered Jung, diddled Miller, and
emerged an idiot,

you love me because required Hi-Flier paper kites, worshiped Rat Fink,
shattered with air rifle my entire Revel airplane collection, gunned
the Royal Norseman, spun the Duncan Imperial, and brandished
the Gordon and Smith, invariably bloodying my lip, crestfallen but
indefatigable,

you love me because I am sharp-tongued, ballistic, gluttonous, sweet,

you love me because I am sentimental, stiff-necked, egotistical, mean,

you love me because I am sacrilegious, sarcastic, defiant, clean,

you love me because I cannot anymore balance on feet nor distinguish human
from animal nor masticate without internal X-Ray image nor
defecate non-visually nor fornicate unselfconsciously nor ignore
hands before sleep—spatulas, paddles—nor enjoy digestion nor

simply anticipate nor conventionally speak nor comprehend speech
nor read without a swimming sensation,

you love me because I am fly bite, wasp sting, branch slap, corner jab, fork
poke, rock gouge, saw rip, lip crunch, paper slice, splinter pierce,
glass slit, outlet shock, pot handle scorch, chili pepper testicle,
thumb smash, hook stuck, door thud, toe stub, Carl Dryer, Agnes
Varda, Bertrand Tavernier, Ingmar Bergman, Robert Bresson,
Jean Cocteau, Michelangelo Antonioni cineaste and literary
insufferable,

you love me because I am Odysseus, Sinbad, Vasco de Gama, Napoleon
Bonaparte, Sir Walter Raleigh, crybaby, whiner, atheist, Sylvester
Cat, Wyatt Earp, Natty Bumpo, My Little Margie, without blemish,
limitation, or extinction, experimental, spontaneous, angry, fixated,
and blind,

you love because I am sensual, aromatic, enveloping, androgynous,

you love me because mother died of failed kidneys and my eyes bad stitches
through which lemon juice flows, and I am inexhaustible,
inextinguishable, incorrigible, incorruptible, martyr, messiah,
impresario, and believer in own lies,

you love me because I whoop and shriek and splash into cold ocean like a
kid, table covering and uncovering chest, foam clicking, horizon
rocking like ship, shout and bounce, glee, eyes glittering, paddle
into swell, seawater gushing mouth, giggling, look at me! look at
me! child tearing off inhibition, enthralled, pelicans like platoon
of towels scudding across ragged sky, complete absorption and
forgetfulness of breast, embarrassment of sixty-two year old
unawareness all day on float, dimensionless, vaporized, beyond
continuum, unconscious, infinitely huge though grain-small,
incorporeal, sunburnt, hairless, frail, and afterward heaven-red-to-
blanket-black the inevitable re-materialization and the profound
intensifying loneliness of comprehension,

you love me because I am breath and heat and touch from a dead body,

you love me because cocaine salts my son like a mackerel, mouth filled, eyeballs

covered, doing time in Connecticut for larceny, liver plugged with Hep C,
veins collapsed, asshole reamed by prostitution, a caught packed twitcher
dying slowly in a boat hold, a naïve delusional ruined man bled white of
beautiful rage, because the concept "broken heart" is a ridiculous fairytale
poeticism for a saturating holocaustal spiritual sickness through which one
eats one's groats, and smiles,

you love me because ahead one point, ninth inning, bases loaded, 3 balls, 2 strikes,
Corpus Christi little league, final batter smashed a grand slam teaching me
in steel cleated shoes and purple cap one of life's cruel weeping lessons:
victory ungraspable by hair's breadth and the indifferent inaccessible
unsympathetic Autocrat,

you love me because Lucy, Fraser, Raymond, Bea reduce me to tub of quivering jelly,
as Skelton mother before me and Allen her mother before her, a family of
tickle bone suckers, owned as easy as sex or breath or milk or tears,

you love me because I am on a labyrinthine university campus dashing through libraries,
classroom buildings, language labs, museum chocked with dusty taxidermy,
hallways, administrative offices late for class I am scheduled to teach, lost
and without proper materials, panicky, ashamed, students undoubtedly
impatiently waiting, I failing to perform duties, metaphorically stripped,
I am in biology lab, cavernous sanctuary, law school stacks, mathematics
department each working predictably and efficiently, only I striding through
in semi-starched slacks am lost, confused, and comical, I your husband
bursting to urinate, underwater blur, plagued by shoelaces and green lizards,
because a ship glides across my window on flood of unknown origin,

you love me because I am Animal Farm, Humpty Dumpty, Rock of Ages, can of paint,
Tropic of Cancer, railroad spike, Origin of Species, ripe split cantaloupe,
six beverages, eighteen nails, twelve broken wheels, infinity of tongues,
half dozen wrenches, influenza, silver gibbon, nineteen dinner rolls, and a
bucket of busted imbroglios,

you love me because when he shoved me sprawling down stairs to playground dirt
scattering textbooks I blurted "thank you" to sixth-grade monster Mickey
McGee, "thank you," with bloody palms smearing chest and butt, because
prior to beating me insensate jeering "Jew, fucking Jew" I reasoned with

thugs, "you don't even know me," and threw not one retaliatory
punch and awoke swollen-eyed in crashing surf, "don't even
know," because evil exists elsewhere, in blunt remote regions
among unutterable barbarians, never among comforting neighborly
faces, and I Ward Cleaver and Darrin Stephens marching,
marching, disbelieving, a copy of Ulysses tucked under shoulder,
you love me because I am God, Necrophiliac, Marcus Aurelius, Joseph Stalin,
Jimmy Jones, Sun Myung Moon, David Koresh, Judah Maccabee,
King Ahasuerus, Rory Calhoun, Pinky Lee, Freddie Freeloader,
Gomez Addams, Mr. Wizard, Captain Marvel, Hiroshi Teshigahara,
Sugar Pops Pete, Craig Breedlove, Xena Warrior Princess, I am
also Hopalong Cassidy in penitentiary garb reading Vladimir
Nabokov atop Topper the Horse outside Jawbone, Arizona, under
gathering November skies, beside a derelict Spanish galleon
resembling brontosaurus pelvic bone and rib cage shot through
with sword grass crawling with lizards,
you love me because a non-institutionalized traumatized un-insulated boy
filmed by hidden corner cameras at bedtime, and atop blanket after
school, invariably on right side in quasi-fetal position soothingly
yet compulsively rocks head back and forth with eyes closed until
asleep, we hypothesize it thrilled like a plummeting roller coaster
while warding off unspecified catastrophes or transported him to a
nourishing bosom, preventing the horror of wakefulness in the cold
prison of loneliness,
you love me because insects cover me like a mitten: flesh flies, bottle flies,
black flies, mosquitoes, arachnids, milkweed bugs, cuckoo
wasps, leafhoppers, water striders, zebra bugs, scorpion flies,
crickets, mites, shrunk tight like heavy boiled cotton, running,
black sawing sheets swarm behind, I am gnawed, stung, bitten,
chewed, implanted, sucked, buried into, egg-hatched, alive, I float
in mist, cringe, am blue-black, blind, ineffectually I swipe clean
crack, wave bear-like appendages, curse my recompense, my sin-
penitence, like scales fingernails curl up and off, I inhale gossamer

hard bodies, beetles, hanging thieves, cow killers, daring jumpers
which sting my entrails, I slap them, they shift, dig deeper, plagued
punished sugar-beast, host, Dante's rung reserved for those of
eternally eaten sweet meats condemned to implore King to say
whether this be eternal damnation for evil done or reward for
extraordinary tenderness,

you love me because I plop head, face down, into ice cream tub, nose wedged,
immersed mouth vacuuming, licking as though it were woman
only richer, creamier, orgiastic, ecstatic, brain reeling, stomach
throat-jumped, cookie dough face mold, Phish Food, Chunky
Monkey, semi-soft receiving chin, lips, forehead bone, blood
numb from frozen crystal, absolute zero, profligate, degenerate,
ploughed-under, white Russian, rum raisin, slurring words like a
substance hit, Kahlua brownie, balls rolling under half shut lids in
overdose back-alley shattered-glass stupor, dragging home to you
ashamed, apologetic, and incorrigible,

you love me because I am mercurial, preemptory, exasperated, menstrual, fork-
cut-able, flaky, immersed,

you love me because I am entity breakable of itself, therefore, entity reparable
of itself, independent, harbor-like, protective, accepting, pond-
still, capable of self-castigation in un-nameable guilt, narcissistic
blame, egocentric loathing, the oversaturating irredeemable sense
of personal failure involving starvation, gluttony, deprivation,
filthiness, or manic-cleanliness, head in hands, muttering
invocations to God or Beelzebub for intervention-musk, modest
unction, antibacterial gel, conversely acquitting myself like the
march of the innocents, singing doo-wop, and sleeping sleep of the
deceased,

you love me finally and irrevocably because…because I sail frigate and
brigantine and corvette and windjammer and caravel, cutlass in
mouth, head scarf flowing, sun-toughened, excitement-drunk,
hungering for booty, beauty, treasure, power for you, for you,
chest pried open like a greedy cabinet, Mako's jaw, worlds flow

in, exotics, rarities, thrall, naughtiness, raunchy security, dirty
bare feet and scabby wealth, your privateer, your picaroon, raged
with derring-do, spilling to your toes intellectual rubies and super-
sensual plums day upon day, showcasing new slash-wounds,
because wind snaps canvas, and you matted on all fours before
pantry weeping, how long can this last, how long can this last,
I love you like the other side of a penny.

I MAKE LOVE to death, she's the lubricated delicious fully-fleshed
apex, thoroughbred ankles, in acrobatic positions we bang
ourselves silly, depleted, requiring slumber, spooning in
moonlight I cup her tits to pond frog sonata, my love whose
totality I cherish, whose fire I swallow, who inflames my plasma,
I gaze at wide infinitude of stars smeared across the sky
like tapioca pearls, sperm chases self toward egg, stinging to
birth billions of deaths, a sumptuous artistic unselfish
creation, The Census Bureau employs my baby who wears
plunge-cut blouse, red vinyl belt, black leather pumps leaving
me home to write messages to God, "the adorable species
crashes against walls like spectacular surf," "I worship
you," "yesterday Consuela birthed Earth's billionth Jesus
who will break his face in a blast furnace factory," "I suck
blew shock raspberry and pickle pepper relish at bone
and soul festival featuring donkey, goat, and clattering
locusts," "I fling milk onto unconscious faces blinking
them awake from hallucinatory histories," we make multi-
lingual music on sheepskin rug before crackling fire, her
Raphael hips, Michelangelo toes, high pink cheeks,
heaving wide and deep like anaconda snakes swallowing
each other, I am aghast with terminal pleasure as is
she, and scatter syllables over everything, while I detest
the exclamation "ah!" I release it here like a helium
squeak, death my grasshopper, walking stick, resur-
rected cricket whom I worship like a photo of Isadora
Duncan, Lana Turner, Gina Lollobrigida, death loves
me like the chocolate dreidel on the twisted paper
stick, like a kiss, a caramel-chocolate cow, licks me to
a puddle, one cannot love until one loves death and
I love her camel hump and rhinoceros rump and arma-
dillo claw and chimpanzee lip, her bestiary fertility, I
enclose her in chest's thick-walled blanket like ovum,

egg, fragile pulsing oval, baby's crushable head, as
she captures me, each within each, pushing from earth
world's only authentic fleshy-leafed oxygen-filled blossom.

*I*MAGINE WORLD'S most unappealing woman, horse-stampeded face, thistle-covered pate, succubus, incubus, rotted teeth, scabs, boils, warts, fat-pockets, voice like burnt grass esophagus, God flung across her back acid, flesh stink, atrophied spine, palsied muscle, hands rictus squirrel carcasses, claw-cragged, evil, Satanic, homicidal, monkey rump, Jew-hater, Nigger-hater, garbage-crawler, rat-eater, cat-slaughterer, yellow snot pus, buboes, curled brown-streaked toe thorns, rag blower, tissue bit littered piss-acrid vagina, insomnia-bitter, buzzard wattle, hirsute, profane, sallow, enraged, cruel, vengeful, matricidal, patricidal, conniving, sniping, pilfering, hellish, denizen of sewers, gutters, alleys, child sex trafficker, sucker of drunk college swine dick in slimy flats, compulsive interior diatribe, "fuck you piece of shit," "fuck yourself," "climb up my butt," "poof you're cremated," "eat my cunt," "exterminate whole fucking race, drown vermin, gas whole bloody unsanitary breeding pestilential sewer pit cockroaches silverfish leeches wood ticks," imagine world's most twisted monster fantasizing boiling babies and pets, eating bone grease, human paste, treasuring Jew soap and human hair rugs, conjuring Auschwitz calcium piles, eye holes, mouth caves, pelvic bowls, walking stick emaciation awaiting ovens, mothers executed back-of-head by Mauser after watching their screaming children wall-bashed to paste, think of this hell-creature dragging rags, crippled, twisted, swinging poisonous torso down street like dilation & curettage, loveless, callous, heartless, egomaniacal, craven, pornographic, stunned by mortis of compassion, empathy, tenderness, generosity, bitten by vitriolic bile and self-abnegation, wanting to chew off her fingers and blow out her brain and mutilate herself and stuff gut with chemical raw chicken to overflowing nausea and toxify herself with chutes of Borax for her compulsive retaliatory sulfuric misanthropy, she is you, she is you.

PART II

That has made all the difference...

*G*ALLOPED IN pushing aside rivals, snatched bride, declared
deathlessness, breathlessness, magnificence, gaiety, infamy,
delirium, satisfaction, swathed through drooling idiots in
doublets, pantaloons praising buttocks and loins like a
venerable butcher, swept her onto bituminous black pig
small as a flea after leaping into clouds squealing, squiggling,
"beloved," I shrieked, core and fornication, as my draw-
bridge thudded on a bloodbath of lunatics slashing into
wet sandwiches and pickles, for my fabulous sky mansion,
she resembled Phyllis Diller and Imogene Coca with a dime
store wig, blindness is thy stout, and took her forthwith
to lair to lay in hair and amaryllis crotch, to die in dis-
solving particles and specks, white Towncraft, mine, hers
Hanes boxer tops, and a little black waterfall bra toppled
like a clot, yet the day's high strain of whipping and
slaughter closed my eyes into red-gold veins of statues
and monuments but she was my accomplished fact
wheezing like a duchess and so I waked protesting all
manner of things, forthrightness, honesty, nobility, peace,
spiked knuckles against malefactors, majesty, I cracked
walnuts, Macadamias, and a seashell of iced butter all
slid to her nose on a lapis lazuli tray, she squeaked and
rolled over and I slurped the dreary seashell of butter
slicked on three fingers, mouth, and both lobes, it being
a treacherous hospital stretcher, or rather a pillow-top
California king cloud upon which we alternately flooded
and supped, she slivered foot nails, consumed raw beets,
squatted in garden, did the funky chicken, blindness is
thy meat, thy mead, thy sleet, emitted from chest pink
valentine hearts, apricot juice, flocks of white geese,
blacksmith mallet pounding, my Federal Express top flight
Nefertiti, God my witness, my absolution ratchet, let there
be lumens…I split the swarm interrupting the sting and

swept her away on my flea called Horse, kiss her and kiss
her in my cloud-high bower, that has made all the difference.

I GIVE YOU shiny mackintosh, you give me hooded pullover,
I give you lingerie, you give me jockeys, I give you red
scrollwork boots, you give me fleece slippers, I give
you infantilism-socks, you give me razor, I give you
concho belt, you give me satchel, I give you con-
temporary fiction, you give me ceramic mug, I give
you chocolate kisses, you give me glass penguin, I
give you oatmeal soap, you give me Pinnocchio, I
give you schefflera, you give me fleece mittens, I
give you violin, you give me wristwatch, I give you
Northern China, Iceland, the Maldives, Venice,
Italy, you give me two-hundred thousand sacrificial
warriors riding beautiful horses, the Russian
throne, ambition, invincibility, I give you coronation,
emerald, ermine, spices, a palace capacious as
Taj Mahal, pillows stuffed with celestial spume,
you give me whales, elephants, falcons, camels,
the Mariana Trench, Mt. Kilimanjaro, I give to
you satin-lined box filled with Andromeda, the
festooned dirigible, the Magellanic Cloud into
which to thrust hands and splash upon face like
luminous milk, God's dreams, infinity's mauve
watercolor, you give me the corner into which
cosmos slams and crashes back upon itself
in raging coils of blood and pulse, and, like an
eyeball dropped into hand, the still point of the
whirling mass, I give you immortality, thrall,
reunion with the dead, the mirror-plated shield
discarded at castle's gate by the exalted knight
who no longer requires it, you give me six
trembling veined-wrapped tears from life's
apical seam tumbling through eternity, each
one striking earth like a sac giving birth.

*W*HEREAS LUST masquerades as romantic love and pounces accordingly,

whereas power masquerades as lust,

whereas unborn babies masquerade as power,

whereas immortality masquerades as unborn babies,

whereas hubris masquerades as immortality,

whereas god masquerades as hubris,

whereas fear masquerades as god,

whereas hot lovers copulate like boiling water, release sperm, swallow sperm,
squeeze sperm, lock sperm in flexed muscle,

whereas I blow myself off my sperm as if off a stretched wire, crumpled waste
wadded beside released essence, dry husk,

whereas my eyes blink open, resurrected, roseate, love,

whereas the humble little broad-back ant-lion throwing from its conical tip gran-
ules ground powder-fine to trap and drink its hapless victim, the juice
and pap fueling another day of eggs and hatching, unacknowledged
exultation,

whereas false prophets like stinking viscera hang on spikes pounded into cross-
beams designed along span of human form in extremis, feet over-
lapped, arms outstretched, Olive or Cedar of Lebanon strong enough,
jammed into earth, to withstand liars, weight of lies,

whereas humankind with its monumental brain, its unfathomable circuitry—sol-
id fuel rocketry, Jaguar supercomputer, Spirit Stealth Bomber—would
dissolve into infantile debauchery, brick of vipers—execution, for-
nication, banditry, incest, drunkenness, accidental death by crystal
meth—were truth disclosed, that love is a lie, innumerable nailed up
god-effigies to symbolize humility, forbearance and a whole exciting
new professional trajectory,

whereas punishments abound—lethal injection, electricity, eternal ice, acid of
ulcer, Sinai lunatic, Eternal Prosecutor, jackboot pastor—to enforce
loving kindness, to push love like meat through our bursting skin, to
sizzle us in love on a superhot skillet till we split our edges into hosan-
nas and hallelujahs and kisses of a hand or emerald or hem,

whereas I love you with all my fear, grandiosity, cold gin fizz in chilled steel

flute, voluptuary, fetishist, sophisticate, bastard—and come for your
wet receptivity, yourself an epicurean stuffed with pan-seared duck of
fear, neither inferior nor superior, one of us—running, dodging, flinch-
ing, shifting—terrified of nothingness, from our pumping processing
sheaths the final plunge and withdrawal of the ruthless lovely sword of
breath,

whereas from the mounted ceiling above your bed my arms extend to raise you
up or deliver down from the cloudy roof like a newborn child onto
your milk and warble and coo, no bigger than a thumb or blasting cap,

whereas I am dumb blind crazy about you, love-wasp stung, welted, burning,
without balm, screaming at fence post, in-sucked, puckered, all glue
and fluid, mad as fireman, ax-bladed, prayer-less, dashing with extin-
guisher over flame-throw, insane, love's yellow-green emission from
nodule, everything and nothing, rich as King of Finland, songful, wild
riot love, I the up-thrust, I the down-push, I the primeval, I the sea
trench, I Poseidon electrified, my purple trident, I love thee nonplussed,
shoeless, hands breast-folded, arranged yet kestrel both screaming
heaven, radioactive without god or Briggs & Stratton or Kawasaki,
welded into you like car collision, crumpled grille, rear view mirror
grafted to eyes, amour, love, biscuit, seaweed bulb, cherry pie, my—
how prosaic—honeybunch, baby cakes, let us pray, and I wade waist
deep in Mediterranean blue to kiss you kiss you kiss you, lake-surface
the magician's blade halving and reuniting me to spontaneous maniacal
applause,

whereas I mailman, greeting card salesman, mineralogist, puppeteer,

whereas alligator love from neighborhood canal attacks wire haired terrier,

whereas this time Tom eviscerated Jerry, Sylvester fricasseed bird screaming for
Granny loopy on Drambuie and Internet porn,

whereas I love you in canoe, in skiff flat shoes, in polished mahogany ribs, in
cowboy lariat, in toreador pants, in pink platypus socks, in rocket ship
nose cone, in black sand Maui, in pink lizard plums, in Tolstoy wedge,
on pterodactyl's spine swooping to Antibes, in bolo tie and concho
belt, in chartreuse aperitif, in thistledown tears, in protested or stroked

smooth cat fur, and more and more and so much more I plop apart
at belt loops, these my fears: castration, sleeplessness, incarceration,
extinction, and abandonment by you to plate of eggs, mosquitoes, and
the tick-tock breath-clock,

whereas rage cloaks love, lies cloak rage, smiles cloak lies, profit cloaks smiles,
and draping profit edge-to-edge like The Bijou velvet curtain hubris
hubris hubris, grizzly talker, hurricane slayer, free scaler, solo nautical
globe circumnavigator, idiots all through whom death fires the ultimate
orgasm, such as Jake who creamed a cliff-face on nylon wings,

whereas like nocturnal, crepuscular, carbuncle, and incubus protrude from my
left ear like a woody cancer, love spins like a plastic dancer on its mu-
sic box mirror wherein avalanches, cataracts, earth-fractures, eruptions
inseminate brain and liquefy heart sucking me into quicksand luscious-
ness through which I flow which flows through me,

whereas unction or unctuous or unctuousness or punctilious or uxorious or
usufruct or usurious,

whereas patriotic flags may fly, confetti, bassoons, balloons, marching bands
celebrating world championships or military victories, love noses in
like two skunks gnashing the gizzard and slurping the chicken, backs
arced, tails dragging, a tin can bangs the nubbins alive, he systems ana-
lyst, she dental hygienist, both saucer-eyed at the little creatures under
the spasm window in yellow moonlight stippled by trees, somewhere
celebrants overturn cars in wild ecstasy and whales smash green water
and elk neck receives the missile, skunk faces are sweet and delicate
and their tongues are beautiful,

whereas wallaby pouch carts young human arm dreaming of dictionaries,

whereas you're hunk of burning love, Venus in blue jeans, heaven's missing
angel, pony tailed Mona, cookin' good lookin', glory of love, soul and
inspiration, pretty woman, dream lover, always and forever, eternally
mine, till poets run out rhyme, until die, no wind no rain, wherever you
are, ooh baby baby, life holds one guarantee, till I kissed you, out of
my head, higher and higher, sugar pie honey, fall to pieces, thrill me
kiss me, crazy, smoke, blind, outa head, unchained, moon vacation,

54

only you, I ache like squeezed lemon, empty flagon of wine, wrench,
screw driver, metal file, wood plane, Johnny get livid, I want to die, ar-
bitrariness, caprice, implacability, dictatorship, the smiting hand, hello
Chantilly calendar stranger, sweeter than love's ten commandments,
never, never, never,

whereas salamander, alligator, lizard, frog, yellow bumpy throat, horned, scaly,
smooth, mudpuppy, olm, conger, peacock, siren, newt, well, incorrigi-
ble and uncorrectable slamming wedge-footed down slide shattering
faces, if love is splendid, time is carbon monoxide, let there be wood
screws, lag bolts, steel cable rope for the party of bandits and hooli-
gans, thieves and miscreants, Swedish meatballs and miniature cheese
pies,

whereas pheasant-love electrifies air with iridescent hues,

whereas dog-love snorts earth with quivering nose,

whereas zebra-love photographs scrub with lazy eyes,

whereas cricket-love waxes sound with polished legs,

whereas sailfish-love freezes beads with whipping tail,

whereas oyster-love fogs ribbon with spurting squirt,

whereas bullfrog-love smudges mud with squatting mush,

whereas hummingbird, scorpion, peacock, duiker, aardvark, beaver, gorilla,
alligator, amoeba, shark,

whereas sloth-love excruciates clocks with riven spines,

whereas my gyroscope balances on your gyroscope like butterflies mating,
daddy's a word I've rarely heard, daddy look, daddy run, daddy please,
daddy what is three times eight, daddy speak, and I word I less often
say, daddy sleep, daddy eat, daddy exercise, daddy keep, gyroscopes
upon gyroscopes Teflon brave, singing and leaning, humming and
flinging, dicing beams, I have l slipped the surly bonds of earth and
danced the sky on laughter-silvered, let us like the anesthetized patient
pray, and touched the face of, the face of, the face of,

whereas should I predecease you about your death—your claim and decomposi-
tion—like a pre-recorded voice spoken from beyond, I wish to scream
upward at sky where He purportedly resides, I wish to scream—

mouth-foaming no doubt—about the extinguishment of such decency, quirkiness, warm-heartedness, and charm, "you worthless fucking piece of shit douche-bag, scum-bucket cock-sucking son-of-a-whore fuck-butt, penny dreadful fifth-rate ass-wipe pant-waist, murderer, coward, imposter, fake, slime-ball, baby rapist, lily-livered filthy flotsam, nobody, nonentity, nothing, zip, I spit in your face, defecate on you, violate your house, tie you up, flay you like a skunk, eat your liver, I crater with a sledge your empty vacuous desiccated skull, waste material, bat guano, bilge-bastard, I excommunicate you to the dry ice glacier for obliterating this woman, for touching one hair on her beautiful head, for desecrating her life, jump up my ass, you blunt-headed, puke-faced, twice-aborted succubus."

*A*S WEDDING vow I super glue shut my eyelids, top-to-base,
soldering lashes, fill ears, shove up urethra tapered tip,
squeeze, liquid-nail tongue to palate, pour concrete gum-
drops over fingertips, dry I click like the ice-encased
tree, cannot hear, see, taste, nor into you ejaculate,
have over-brimmed nostrils, am pure spirit, every sense
numb—god of bodilessness oblivious to your texture,
expression, piquancy, face, am thickly opposite to, for
instance, Barbara "Hello Stranger" Lewis's oozing
eroticism, prefer after self-sacrifice to unhook bone
from excitation, blood from exhilaration, brain from
hallucination, as wedding vow I obliterate tactility with
tube called Gorilla, would have you too open mouth,
ply vagina, entomb lids, I have known unendurable
craziness: compulsion, grandiosity, monomania,
fixation, brain spewing jellyfish, I eliminate excruciation
by thrusting dick into wet quickset, flooding tongue,
clogging auditory faculty, as wedding vow I pour us
into isolated impenetrable blocks, rendering us un-
corruptible, plowing under the marriage bed, the
proclamation, prattle and grunt, the irremediable
implication resulting in discord and alienation, annihil-
ating eternally the perennial bruise and the annual
cleave, for wedding vow immobilize earthly gratify-
cation, whereupon our transfiguration, as wedding gift,
the intermingling in each other like congenial breezes.

I HEMOPHILIAC LIE beside you Cruetzfeldt-Jakob Disease and
kiss you like a budgerigar, bed sheets rustle, ice stars
twinkle, I slide sickle cell anemia like buttery silk under
quivering Ataxia Myxoma and nibble your shoulder like
a walnut piece, car lights race along ceiling, Wolff-
Parkinson-White Syndrome lays you down like a heavy
feather and I raised on stalks and palms lick quivering
Guillaine-Barre-palsied nipples like a split-tongue
crow stricken with Nuclear Factor Kappa B Essential
Modulator Disease, your thighs open soundlessly like
sashes—no sprockets, wheels, or cogs—and I am there
Von Willebrand, Thalassemias, Lymphocytopenia
balled into one glorious oblivion of squish and slide,
two heaving adults in love's having, heavily betrothed,
wet sand flesh in the ochre Gambrel, mid-February,
ice fangs hanging, you with Crohn's Disease, I with TB
rheumatic heart, chronic obstructive pulmonary
hypertension, like three aces with the two queens of
anorexia-nervosa and body dysmorphic dysfunction
plying muscular love like a smokin' rock drummer,
and your supraventricular pericarditis splashes
oxygenated blood against cellophane walls rapturous
rapturous like a dozen monkeys howling in green
canopies and I with the dual painted eggs of lymph-
oma and myoepithelial carcinoma of the parotid
gland ecstatically slam into a doubled-over bubbling
giant sea clam screaming lymphangioleiomyomatosis.

I AM VALUABLE to the extent that I assuage other people, were
I a household object it would be the sponge, saturate me,
wring me, others' tears weep from my holes, in this I am
a magnificent lover, depression overwhelmed my men
whom I relieved, I slide to knees to play the subjugated,
the dominated, swelling his ego like a king, I play
chambermaid and cordon bleu chef enveloping him in
gastronomical bliss of open pot lid—potato leek stew,
lime-rubbed chicken, he stretched on couch like a
caliph awaiting his meat which in silk slippers I serve with
sweet yogurt drink, I am the genetically predisposed
savior of special needs children, and in that capacity
earned my doctorate in education to serve the dyslexic,
autistic, borderline personality, ADHD, arriving home
from work each night spill-heavy for overnight
wringing that I may soak up tomorrow's suffering, I
could have been a 17th century geisha, courtesan, or
lady in waiting, a minor-key Mother Teresa invisible
save for method of delivery—advocacy or therapist,
or mentor—what difference, only a saint could love
the selfless, the congenital caregiver over-lain by
tedious cyclical saturation and depletion, I ask you
anyway to possess me with madness and ferocity.

I **FLY MY** tumor from Albuquerque to Boston, marriage and the Dana Farber Institute Carnival cruise where surgeon excises right salivary gland, other newlyweds buy Florence, we tour with love-protestations pre-op and recovery room, "my goddess," anesthetized I protest, "eternally," "most wonderful," cheek caved, baseball stitches, drain bulb, magical mind drug, might as well be *L'Escargot,* roasted brill with Jerusalem artichoke cream, chilled Pinot Gris, but this is thiopentone sodium and halothane those wonderful delicacies and I floating dreamily, what better reason for middle age people to legalize union than to cheat insurance companies, to piggyback the one in need of treatment—parotidectomy, hospitalization, radiotherapy—on the other's family plan, zero deductible, total expenditure from cancer-to-emission fifteen dollars, and a wife in the deal whom I love more intensely than I love my tumor's disappearance, forever hence to mate like eagles, in mid-air, connubiality on cancer ward between Mr. Sutton atwist in drip tubes and Ms. Blassingame's gaping upper palate, like a Caribbean Island cruise, strolling with IV drip-stand warm white sand, un-tan, arm-in-arm, past nurse's station and fellow prostrate vacationers, this, too, is beautiful, drain tubes, colostomy bags, laryngectomy hole, craniotomy drill, the gingerly halting waltz down love's squeaky aisle, marriage in Massachusetts, December, two-thousand seven, two gratified humans, one critically ill, at their moment of glory, exchanging vows.

I **LOVE YOU** because you reflect my insanity—
defensiveness with defensiveness, paranoia
with paranoia, insecurity with insecurity,
you accuse my accusation as accusatory,
infinity of facing mirrors, "I am so…" you
finish my statement, "infuriating," and thus
we travel in love's vehicle, seized by my
obsessive-compulsive thought you perform
the ritual, incapable of distinguishing source
from echo, hullooooh! one shouts into
mountain range, hullooooh! with equal
intensity one answers, you love me because
I am you transgendered, penis-slit split,
peeled back into vagina, your vagina
ridged with steel-hard penis with whose
authority you employ to penetrate me,
misidentification in the kitchen where our
liquids intermix in one deranged continuous
wheel, I compliment your omelet which I
created gratifying you who are me, I
jiggle with giddiness which is yours,
at night we swallow each other's pills.

*Y*OUNG MALE sexually plunges female for the unborn child,
to suck it from theory into flesh like a nexus, shovels
himself in to galvanize the love-knot, the blood-surge,
he gathers like rope his creamy throw to lasso and
lash insemination to cave, his implantation—purpose-
ful violence grind mash, young male industry, stinger
and mouth, hive, queen, deep deeper, multiplication,
old male such as I gently hovering like butterfly, study-
ing my slow withdrawal and thrust inside his post-
menopausal wife, her non-ovulating easefulness, mouths
need not bite hickeys into hollows but crawl, like snail,
ribcage smearing mournful muttering prayer, doors
in a column infinitely long sequentially open in old
man's mind, each revealing, like dark mirror images,
exhausting previous incarnations spilling inaudible
apologies upon lover's breast, young male with
thoroughbred thighs batter-rams upon his first door
for profitable sowing while young female arcs back
to him to answer the call screaming down ether,
to unleash the haunting demanding scream from
its remotest hall and yank it through intensified
bowler like a magic rabbit, young male and female
boiling over like porridge pot sting the world
with urgent mash of shaft and lips, old such as
we infused with levity in seizure linger, equivocate,
helium hands bouncing lightly over sternum or
knee like birthday balloon, giggle now in soft
repose at the easeful acquisition of pure leisure.

H E REALIZED today, suddenly and unpredictably, that he does not know how to love, that practically all relationships fail, that schools do not teach love, nor is desire or predilection sufficient, that idealized love portrayed in storybook, mythology, and legend is mirage, delusion, and artifice, further he understood that religion is an avaricious syndicated criminality holding at ransom for preeminence and social supremacy souls kidnapped from owners, hypocritically and ruthlessly postulating like the jolly benevolent patriarch, the wrathful but forgiving God concocted to crush and control human spontaneity along a slick franchised business model, that the entire autocracy and enterprise constitutes a violence and lie, an inner beating undetectable on flesh the way beating a woman with a pillowcase filled with oranges leaves no evidence, he realized unexpectedly that he is a loveless, Godless man inculcated the reform Jew—Hebrew school, Bar Mitzvah, confirmation—who is now at sixty-two in marriage number four, but who too often feels dead and atheistic, or too rarely electrified and pietistic but who nevertheless persists, lifts spoon to salivation, eliminates, attends events, selects shoes, performs with middling competency the life-sustaining exercises, and is often gratifyingly libidinous, as homo sapiens with its unique trans-seasonal continuous coitus is, a species universally psychologically damaging round-clock reproductive conflagration and clanging bell, like the dance marathon brutalizing physically vigorous contestants, finally irreparably annihilating spirit, he realized today sometime after hotcakes that Earth is a granule and that human but its microscopic inhabitant arrogant, ego-filled, mightily striving for nothing, but that strive it must, for microscopic starvation is starvation and microscopic love is love and both feel massive and nonnegotiable and deliver ego, dominance, satisfaction, glow, crow is after all crow, sheeny, fine, rooster is rooster, and man is man with hobbies, symbols, emblems, and codes, he awaits the morning he will suddenly, without warning realize that this meager apportionment is part and parcel love and God, that this faithlessness, despair, dizziness, uncertainty—this horrifying loneliness—is the essence of beauty, humility, and organismic connectedness and that his ability to imagine this possibility foreshadows—guarantees—that he will awake one day—undoubtedly soon—to this revelation filling his marrow with joy and inspiration.

I SCRATCH NOSE, *you scratch nose,* we imitate, I yank lobe, *you yank lobe,* protrude tongue, *protrude tongue,* wiggle toes, *toes,* I plant fist on hiked hip, *you plant fist on hiked hip,* hop, *hop,* pout, *pout,* I, Simon, lead, with right hand I describe overhead halo, simultaneously with left pat tummy while counting to ten, mirror-like you mimic, two monkeys, I step toward, pucker, kiss, *you pucker likewise,* I back-of-hand wipe mouth, *you wipe mouth but, disobediently, with opposite hand,* right-to-left I jump, *left-to-right you jump, wicked, insubordinate,* I am angry, tap floor with toe, rock foot backward, *you tap heel, jump sidewise,* I slap, *you offensively indignantly slap,* I want reconciliation and with sad clown-face stick forefinger into right ear like a pistol barrel symbolizing despair, surprisingly *precisely you obey,* I love you and with feet nailed to floor acrobatically fall backward onto palms staring at back wall, stomach arched like Utah, *you like rubber muscle and bliss bend backward likewise,* I push off feet, stand on hands, spring upright, *you repeat but, as if to drumroll, tack on somersault,* furious at insolence with muscular right leg I kick steel dog dish splashing water against your shin, *insubordinately you hurl at me cantaloupe-half streaking wall,* outraged like a troop-defied sergeant I bark commands, follow, perform, comport, obey, optimistically with spread fingers I form a junior birdman mask, *you blow raspberries like a mad cockatoo, swing round and recede,* alone in terrifying solitude, red dawn, long shadows, I ponder my failure, lack of tenderness, veiled misogyny, misappropriation of superior strength, volume, hypocrisy, and the luge-chute of pride, postage

72

stamp female sexual and societal infantilism, puffed
out still but uncoordinatedly, like a snapped crusta-
cean, back to you I clatter wordless, interplanetary,
magnetically disabled, and stuffed with contrition.

*F*ACING EACH other we open chests cavity, slip arms through arms, tie
sleeves round back and become each other's straight jacket, as
if sheet-metal wrapped, two terrified humans lashed, mouths to
each perpetually pressed, this is powerful imagery, the only
trenchant marriage-metaphor, mutually accepted sexual liberties
eat Becky and Finn, like battery acid, a stench of openness hangs
in their air, union as orgy, we twist cuffs like tourniquets creaking
stiff fabric while Larry sucking liberation-theology cracks like a plastic
mannequin, visionary marital progressives embracing the moral
equivalency of criminals, hallucinatory heads full of cake-froth
and invincibility, the annihilated thing cannot simultaneously exist,
we have no clasps down the front, her arms slid through mine
knotted round back in one sweeping stretch, discipline, discipline,
eternal kiss, ribs in marbled flesh, rare, interlocked, inextricable,
sweet, while revolutionaries disappear in private holocausts.

*B*ECAUSE YOU are pretty and delightfully flighty, because your spine is a string of pearls, because you're slacked like Phyllis Diller, because you have Venus Fly Trap eyes, because your fingers photosynthesize, because irregular inviting teeth, because pouty breasts like chastened child, because nature created outie, because blonde filigree cuts across brow, because cool smooth ass and marble thighs, because tootsie pop thumb to suck all night, because bracketed mouth and facial lines, because high foot arches and kernel corn toes, because wide hip voluptuousness and feathered pubic mound, because submissive bashful flitter, because skinny bookish fingers remember throat of violin, because honor poses undue risk to mind and flesh, yet you plunge into life's tempestuousness, because rose skein, quinoa steam, shutter-click, page-flip, heart-split, voice-crack, clasp and press monolith to cleaving breast leaving martyrdom to confessionalists, rigidity to smelting vats, self-flagellation to medievalists, original sin to penitents you are my (hackneyed, predictable, cornball, clichéd term of endearment.)

PART III

Baby, baby can't you hear my heartbeat...

*T*HE ONES who cannot live without the other, man who blows out
heart, woman who drowns in vodka, husband who commits
murder-suicide, mother who careens off cliff into lake, over-
dosed coed, sophomore crashing Honda, homosexual hanging
self, housewife gassing face, matron eating herself diabetic,
cocaine, handgun, shotgun, needle, razor, clothesline, anti-
convulsion pills, guru ignites gasoline, bankrupt businessman
eats pistol muzzle, others who simply kiss attrition, helpmate
of years discarded for secretary splashes into darkness,
Shaker disappears under wood plane, Mormon sheds cheese-
cloth, soldier re-enlists, poetess marries palomino, matron
applies Cutex to heart polish , yachtsman sails "Dublin Darlin"
into God's fogbank, (but, oh, the hearty ones such as
jilted Trish jitterbugging herself into sweet cream butter),
degraded physicist swallows fuel rod, movie icon garrotes
self, weight-belted scuba instructor, frozen naked Alaskan,
mercury ingested pharmacist, mademoiselle acetamino-
phen ad infinitum, doomed wing-walker, glissading ice
climber, self-sabotaged parachutist, grizzled cop, "ain't no
sunshine," "tears on pillow," "leader of pack," "only lonely,"
"baby baby can't you hear heartbeat," cries the future
suicide, "teardrops in coffee," but worse, viricide, filicide,
if you abandon me—this is mapped—I would drink Subaru's
carbon monoxide in Plainfield, Mass. where we live on
4.5 acres of old growth forest inhabited by porcupine, bear,
deer, tank calibrated to empty fast providing me a quiet
aftermath, though I could conceivably rip the tube, punch
the remote, burst out my tomb into sun, rent clothes, roll
in dust, and bawl with hurt—I care that much, or so I think.

*P*RINCE ACHMED dashes about seeking a suitable mate, failing in Alhambra, mounts magic horse, flies to Qataban, Abu-Abu, Alexandria, no princess presents, slaps horse's horn for Wadi Quadiash: nothing, zilch, pinching beast's rump returns home to join Match.com, Babes.org, and Russianbrides.edu, big-tit opportunities but disheartening—usual slush pile—mounts magic goat which bores through granite to Eldorado, naked woman alcoves, Ginger fascinates, Clarissa flicks Bic, burrows sidewise to substrate Mesopotamia replete of barefoot brunettes with oil slick eyes—deep black mirrors—scores a piece, but still zip, blows on *Magnifique's* neck who like industrial screw-drill surfaces into his barley syrup kitchen where stuffs on warm nougat, mentally maps his princess: honey blonde locks brushing backs of knees, alabaster flesh splashed with speckles, dainty arches, tiny tummy pooch, valentine lips, waxed pubis, virgin, nibble-delicate ears, behind closed eyes conjures her nude and ready, frenzy-whipped again mounts beast for enchanted Shangri-Las beside cobalt green seas and cornflower blue hills, eats flaky pastry inside thatched gazebo and giant bivalve shell, whorehouses each, just voracious soulless opportunistic ghastly bitches in dungeon-dens bleeding copulation and cannibalism, a stinking world, Achmed craves simultaneously incest and suicide, nobody bests Mother—sweet Pinarsade— with sensual dimples, in terminal despair, in deprivation's crushing fist man hallucinates his exit, under mosquito net on Achmed's bed a scorpion appears in whom he hallucinates his voluptuous maid naked and free surrounded by cedars of Lebanon, fig trees, vineyards and forsythia buds, and he kisses and kisses and gets big and stiff and she stings him with love and stings him with vision and stings with him tongue and comes and comes, and he falls back in spectacular ecstasy.

*B*EAMING, YOU present a steaming confection: summer squash,
sweet potato, carrots, lamb, turmeric, chili powder, butter,
cumin, an aromatic stew, offering all in a glazed clay bowl as
if offering The Transfiguration, proudly, shoulders back, this
splendor we enjoy with Bengal tea and chilled rice pudding,
any idiot can combine genitals, but only lovers climax food.

I CAN FEAR no more and surrender to love, I pull to hate, being male, all rivals, deride, ridicule, buffoon in ridiculous brogues, lunatic nicotine sucker, tattoo wonder, crucify Hawaiian-printed vacationing glad-hander, slavish fool of flaming ego fated for anonymity under crappy headstone memorializing zero, two Beaver Cleaver sons slated for sleaze, females sacrosanct whom, goddesses, I worship and deserve, at will possess with irresistible word, crooked finger, appear! submit! I superior to male stumblebums, dilettantes, but as I said, I fear no more and capitulate to love, miraculous humanity, preciousness under hair plug, J Press suit, tan tortilla tam, the preposterous im-ponderable platypus mystery of improbable humanity, each life in-estimable, invaluable, the sand-shovel-pail paradigm, the Tonka truck syndrome, marriage, coupling, reproduction, accumulation, jubilant, melancholy, revived, triumphant, heaving for breath on expiration bed, blunted, incapacitated, lowered into pit, well, the nobility of it all, the divinity, loving easy as floating on a shoal, rippling wavelets smooth as stone, the abandonment of hatred—abeyance, disbursement—the fatiguing ceaseless other pummeling resulting in self-contamination, I love her, I kiss her bridge, I sweeten tea, I love shore caster, day laborer, tool dye man, financial district wizard, chameleon and king, fried chicken champion, sushi connoisseur, herring-mackerel rancher, I love real estate developer, pleader of cases, professor, pontificator, demagogue, dog, publisher and politician, for today is the day I lay in cool water, baptized, mouth-breathing, posteriorly sub-merged, thankful, forgiven, human vessel gaping for stranger, open for business, acid and rancor neutralized in tincture, I now sentimentalist, syrup-sappy, after gratifying thunder and profitable rage, dissolve into oblivion like a self-consumed can-nibal, invisible embracer, undistinguished caresser, neophyte.

WHEN MOTHER died I vowed a belief in God, the dead God's clientele, I surmised, ushering souls to Paradise, discarding contemptuous packaging, Benevolent Savior presiding simultaneously over the death enterprises: genocides, epidemics, starvation, suicide bombings, homicides, accidents, wars, the Great Emancipator reclaiming His battered wanderers, but then I contemplated the coterminous life-enforcing miracles: births, survivals, escapes, heroics, refusals, revivifications, and realizing the absurdity of such omnipotence abandoned faith and wept like a citrus for my loneliness, I hungered to sense The Glorious Presence in mother's death room, that intuited and certain Emanation but witnessed nothing but waste, futility, mother's horrible mask and debility, disfigurement and humiliation after all her worldly swirl of adventurism, sexuality, ownership, and recognition, I promised obedience, awe, an overabundant heart, Love is what I vowed in her mausoleum, but tethered—she—to nothingness amidst albeit tender midwives with clipboards and name plates administering the formality of morphine and Benadryl, evidence failed for "the tunnel of light," or Mama arrived to guide her across, nor smile nor glint of eye, no luminous Host, mere biological expiration in artificial space consisting of latex, plastic, vinyl, and cotton arranged in geometric archetypes enclosing today's failed organism, for several days, stunned by the perishable's enslavement to its implacable master I prayed words from my mouth like a party balloon sculptor but collapsed like a deflated proselyte, lungs occluded with laughing gas and out floated God in a series of giggles, a sanity lapse Monday through Friday in March's fat middle, the week of my ecstasy in which I wept saline mirrors, "don't lose that feeling," my wife pleaded, "precious," but I gapped like poorly set putty and slid off the brick, love is a bastard, death a bitch, and life is a dog I obey like a human, oh baby, baby, let's waltz in our glass slippers through the wide white expanse.

*D*ADDY WHO sits in pelvic bowl, 90, dry glue skin, hematomas
like bomb pattern, daddy of bottomless Coco Puff, daddy
pile-driver knuckles gone mush, daddy Florsheim shoe
shuffler, diaper daddy, dizzy daddy, stung brain daddy,
I smash boy-lips against daddy, I lip-smear daddy, weep
and drag, blubber and smudge, I kiss with rage, white
rage love, daddy fascist, vulture-beak god, I crush snot-
nose into hollow, slide down chest, old rot, sour bot,
shitting himself, cataract-blur, sixty chocolate wrapper
wads on one side, eighty on other, where are we, any-
way? I slobber, slide shins to sallow feet, varicose-
shattered, gnarled yellow claws, Biff-sling on them
snot-string, sniveling, daddy love, father love, pro-
genitor love, semen-man gone broccoli—flowering—and
son cratered, leaking whale tears, "I love you," "I love
you," goddamn lousy piece of crap bastard," de-
mented, doughy, fish-bellied fucker, I cram his arm
into my mouth, feed it down, gag and feed, wet it, shove
it, down to gut, gnashing tissue, all-devouring vat-
acid, stuff with him, I had marriages, children, prop-
erties, jobs, but shove him down finally proud, in-
continent pant-stink, Sammy, Rotary, Lion's Club,
BMOC, big macher, and I devastated fatherless child
love-blubbering, I needed, desired—"look at me,"
"check this out!"—praise, acclaim, swell with pride,
I suck his kneecap like mendicant, dry nipple, whole
joint inside, suck suck, and finally buckle, my god,
my God, my decaying lymphatic evaporating God.

I PULL AN actor's plastic skull over my head and clown
about, "I, Death," "kneel before God," "bone stew, mon
amour," *Seventh Seal, Jeanne d'Arc,* maggoty
eye-hollows, I present skinless mouth to kiss, she
presses lips, thespian's dilapidated prop, scraped,
cracked, I feed into me through mouth-hole cake-
wedge and want to fuck—mask affixed—before
a mirror, Caravaggio's "Copulation with Death,"
Botticelli's "Crucifixion of Cleopatra" gilt-framed
Madonna and Death, or Death with Dewey Rose,
bloomed calix, but I yank off skull, we relax, I
unzip, slide off her pants, perform cunnilingus,
supple muscle slurping silky flan, mask dragged
off by mongrel for proper burial, I have the
array of masks for future furor: Satan, Nixon,
Adolph Hitler, but for now pull chicken's greasy
wishbone, and I who wish the granting of her
wish emerge victorious, my pillowy sacrifice,
she complains of jaw pain, "ear infection," I
suggest, or cavity, I grab heating pad, later, all
electronics powered off, snow tapping window-
pane, we peel off all our flesh exposing what
lies beneath, terror or inexpressible happiness.

*L*OVE TEARS off my face, does not stamp new one nor beautify nor make me luminous, it un-faces me exposing nerve, sinew, tendon, bone, hinges, I love you is skin ripped forehead-to-chin, features hanging like a rag, winter stings, summer chafes, struck on love's sandpaper box I scream through night my subcutaneous head, love the naked biological sphere suspended horrifically in open air, I love, therefore, am indistinguishable, nondescript, anonymous, quotidian, blank, l traverse hallways, ignite engine, whisper down corridor of sullen hall, athrob with love, infinitely small, love is no face at all.

I MAKE MYSELF unlovable by eating myself obese, "who could love this?" I grunt and grab handfuls, I self-flagellate, "fat," "disgusting," you strive to disguise revulsion and suck me off, I'm repugnant, deliberately, who loves me gets spiritually ripped and emotionally bashed, like a panic disorder victim, (conversely, consider the successful wunderkind so microscopically self-defined he's terminally befuddled), who loves me my possessive deceased mother eliminates with fingernail, tongue, or teeth—she has employed each—ubiquitous harrowing shadow, meaning I'm hers, this cloud, and eat myself horrible, Double Stuff, Triscuits, Reese's Peanut Butter Cup, I eat breathless, acid reflux, and mewl all night, three-hundred pound grouper, my mouth an enzyme-saturated convulsing intestine through which into vat of insatiability world in chunks drops, outwardly bloat straining pants to bursting so you cannot adore me, my lovers starve themselves in backlash, pelvises wedged, sallow, sick, in psychiatric response, prematurely wrinkle, emaciated, isn't this brutal, almost blackly comical? comedian crammed with ice cream gooped Crisco in apartment house with witless wife, chuckles, guffaws, infectious laughter like chain saw rattle, unsure if tickled or terrified, this is a love song addressing a certain life paradigm, a fearful man subconsciously betrothed to a polished dead witch risen from the crypt to slaughter rivals with bludgeons of butter, sugar, flour, Coke making him grotesque and marvelously avoidable save for she who consumed him young and in whose eye-sockets maggots wriggle.

*D*EATH POLE-DANCES to Nine Inch Nails, dimpled hemispheres, rocket
nipples, psychedelic light-bath, cinnamon candy lips, Death's G-
strap rides vagina, money—crisp laundry—folds over string, Death
flips stiletto into crowd, males tongue it or wedge in sweaty
knuckles, kaboom, kaboom, boom-boom, boom-boom, boom-
boom, Death humps air, air moans, love love love, upside down,
nobody tighter, meaner, creamier, slicker, not Brianna, not
Kimberly, amber sweat glistens her creases, above God I wor-
ship her, above riches, Bugatti, I crave only her tight orgasmic
clasp, locked woman rider, she's not ocean, begonia, forest,
nor tide but intestine, muscle, saliva, and lash, flexed ridges,
immortality's crack-hit, addicted addicted addicted addicted,
none else do I crave, I am desiccation, stomach-gut, dried
rubber cement without her, scalp-fleck on sofa, cat hair,
styptic stick, plastic toilet brush without her wet slurp-slip
baby-breath, Death my cataleptic acrobat who rope-dangles
from my teeth to hers, naked, spinning to primitive drum,
I eat, I bliss, I suck, I flip, I gaze, I drown, I dance, I slash,
she loves me afresh deck after deck, wild cherry scent,
Pantene Blonde Expressions, acrid jungle musk, and then
with kidneys or lymph or brain she gets down to business.

*Y*OU SLAP your ears, shout no-no-no-no-no not to hear
that sister thinks you're a shit and hopes a truck
smashes over you, or that Johnny who doesn't give
fuck got an A in math while you studied off your
ass for a C+, you clueless bloody moron, or that
some predator left Rex's ravaged carcass behind
the trash, you should see his head, ha-ha-ha
what clueless mongrel with his jangling tags and
liver-flavored chunks, no-no-no-no-no slapping
ears, wah-wah-wah, just noise, fog, mother's
dying of kidney disease, Eddie wants divorce,
Jackie whom you love wishes you'd dry up,
take a flying hike, or just make like a tree, *she's*
Bobby's girl, not you, so there, you delusional
megalomaniacal slut, who do you think you
are with your chubby hump and elephantine
nose, we're cleated, never had a snowball's
chance, try geeky Ronnie or crack-head Paul
why don't cha, get Christ out the way, blast
off, spaz, don't you get it, nobody gives a rat's,
walking zero, no thanks, flake off, or batting
ears and chanting la-la-la-la-la-la-la-la-la-la
egomaniacal narcissistic controlling ass in-
capable of intimacy, bastard, fucker, piece
of shit with your faux sensitivity and worth-
less shrink, what have you learned, any-
way, nada, coward, fish, yourself only, you
inviolable superior inaccessible self, flesh-
covered ice, outta here, kaput, go find an-
other gullible desperate love-struck victim
to devastate with your mesmerizing soul-
ful glamorous hypnotic heart-dilating lie.

*R*ULES FOR men: never reveal contentment, appear disgruntled, misanthropic, tortured, seething, appear critical, compress joy to concrete cube, in this internal thick-walled prison bend traceries of bliss back upon themselves creating a dense impenetrable brick, never reveal vulnerability, tenderness, when sexed be mechanical, flip, yank, shove, rip, be intractable, clenched, threatening, stiff, unconquerably fascist, smiles forbidden, never fatten— curl pump jerk lift—emulate the Gelandewagen—luxury fused with lubed practicality, never beat but exude threat, keep walls and cudgels close, ball fists, whisper endearments, encouragements, baby, sweetie, honey, doll creating cognitive devastation, cultivate enigma and insecurity, tearful fear, drive her to abstraction, cosmetics, tweezers, paint, emulate her abusive father, worship and rage, seduction and scorn, intimidatingly big, unpredictable as a cat, devise an insomnia-driven psychological profile, serve her in bed Florentine, latte with hand-picked daisy, brooding, obliquely miffed, "okay?" inquire, "satisfied?" feel forehead, attend, apropos nothing present gifts, garlic press, egg whisk, water color set, carry black intimidating attaché, read aloud to she ensconced in blankets before slumber—women adore this—Babel, Baudelaire, De Sade, O'Conner—work behind closed door, spend one evening per week at "friends night out", or, barring that, dawdle at tavern, off-balancing her, upon return, kiss, "how stunning!" and go to sleep, corollaries: night sweat, torment-dream, demons, suck her in, worry her, make her minister, be nihilistic, self-destructive, harsh, wound yourself, don't dance, never dance, usher her to others' steps, fraudulent twits, take her to Elks to flaunt superiority as aloof adjudicator of others' pedantry—dancers cannot attach, to explode myths eat quiche, kirsch pudding, cliché but riveting, revile spectator sports, sports shrivel pee-pee into pig-tail curl, un-blooded worshipper with pennant and glow stick, but goggled in Speedo swim lean and smooth, or back convex in butterfly stroke, arms out-stretched, water sheeting off bathing cap, sweat on her mechanically, indifferent, take her missionary on chopping block, wad her like garbage you hate to waste, dispose of

her repeatedly, rules for women: pretend—demure—non-omnipotence,
that you—Circe, Medusa, Kyoto Dragon—do not scarlet-clawed
scoop from pit and devour like shrimp male after male, beauty
force-multiplying efficiency, that you do not control decision on
which your man bloodies knuckles, pretend—demure—incompetence
to your helpless whelp by bungling at bowling, knock-kneed,
squealing at bait and cold landed thrasher throwing icky pink-flakes,
feign financial misfit, midget accruing obsequiously to him all
wizardry when brain's in fact a razor-ball of brilliance and
lethality, oh, yes, I see, Tarzan, Sinbad, my Hercules, paint toe
nails tar, mustard, or blood, tattoo ass, spaghetti strap sandals,
the fragile-foot illusion, clippers, dyes, perfume, be trendily liter-
ate, conversant with Didion, Jhabvala, Oates, but ignorant of
Hans Castorp, von Passenow, Peter Kien, play clueless, obtuse,
naïve, depend on him for necessities, be impulsive, illogical,
oblique, men need with hammer and spike to secure ethereality,
wear his long sleeve shirt, bird bony, tiny, naked below tail
minus lacy black panties, swallowed in his robes transmits
helplessness, be small enough to fit in his mouth like a stone,
fail, duff, do not cut your locks, be blushed ovary-box, proud
yet weak, non-aggressively available, spilling like tearful
pail, need man-dominance, men despise independent cunts,
succeed but marginally in female industry: fiber arts, interior
design, dental hygiene comfortable with objectification and
stereotyping of body parts, punch exasperated with thumb-
inside fist your lover's chest, comical, ineffectual, monkey-
like, and accept with grace physical grit, incommunicativeness,
rigidity, storm furiously to friend's house aware you would
die without his love and return midnight contrite with
mascara tracks, worship his tyranny and inflexibility, his
totalitarianism, his false bravado in the murderous machine
of capitalism and competition, the culture of souls cluttering
the beach like washed up trash, be manipulable, sacrificial,

electric-fur alive curling on his tummy like a beaver or
squirrel—all this your charade, your Little Women tableau
by the secret virtuosa, absolute and incontestable, panto-
miming the identity of the dunce and idiot who knows
she's superior, dominant, overwhelming, and indispensable.

I INVENT A DISASTER we must survive: Hurricane Ida howling, peels
roof like K-ration, lashes, tied to toilet with leather straps
we kiss, everything thick pea soup, horizontal rain, picture
window implodes, Chevy bounces on front tires, Ida shrieks
like seventy witches, and we stretched like flags from
base of Toto, shoes up-sucked, suddenly stillness, placid
Summer, baseball lovely, oiled mitt and snow cone syrup,
suddenly reverse rotation razor-sheering and again out-
stretched, joints popping, love-professed and catechized,
absolved of bitterness rancor suspicion failure, promises
blurted between straining ligament, Category 5, and
the approaching snake apocalypse, copperheads, cotton-
mouths, rattlers dropping like bullwhips from rafters,
like intestines from a gutted calf, and you, I, naked-
nippled, dirt-streaked, deltoids clenched like pipe wrench,
then emerging from concrete slab of totaled house
under God's lightly dripping faucet, reproductive again,
carrying within, I, tadpoles of liquid fire, and she, the
ewe's swamp of furious eggs, geneses, vein shot am-
bassadors of massive nations, I fabricate our adventure,
ground zero flash unleashing razor wire of fire and
ash, yammering imprecations, I floor it, pistons ham-
mer, Highway 85, fight/flight happiness, out toxic
mouth of devouring debris cinematically shoots black-
orange hood bird, 120, 125, radio dead, Amargosa
Valley, dog yanking bottom off Coppertone gal, Hamm's
Sky Blue Water, Esso gas, Kennecott Minerals com-
pressed by speed into block of concrete, mountains
approaching, you and I caught unawares in T-shirts
and dungarees, suddenly side-slipping purloined
Cessna before billowing fiery cloud, across Mexico,
Galapagos, Bolivia, Brazil, baby baby, hearts mag-
niloquent, braids of flashing silver streams, suddenly

crashing, engine sputter, up-rushing canopy, platinum
blond curtain covering grime-streaked shoulder, pants
squashing reproductive bang of two adrenalin riven
angels pitching under vengeance-is-mine wrathful
ashen cloud, then down in Ebola ravaged town, lique-
fied guts, maggoty ruts, corpses, grimaces, gruesome
bugs, billowing pyres, you Dale, I Flash careening in
Duisenberg SJ Speedster to secret launch pad, Oh
Flash, flaming river, stink, foul, Stygian epithelium, bone
marrow rot, captain, hero, superman to thee I cling,
3, 2, 1, blastoff! from observation window rioting ants,
black eruptions, slow holocaust, and you and I, in tin-
foil suits spinning like bullet to Axalon, firm of flesh
and quick as lizard, our former world a pus-filled blister.

*O*NCE LIFE'S elixir, life's ambergris, sacred, non-negotiable,
worth risk of ridicule, reputation, honor, pride to get
it, smashed, sober, morning, night, stubble-bearded,
bloodied, mononucleosis-ridden, feverish, just get it
and bask, inflate, megalomaniacal, playing angles,
percentages, smooth operator, intuitive technique,
"hello sexy eyes," "va va voom," bourbon, Coke,
spraying semen like garden hose, tenacious, in-
discriminate, lacerating self on hormonal edge,
calumnious bile, lies, conceit on this exhilaration-
globe replete with opportunities: motel, dorm
room, frat house, back seat, platforms of seduction,
stages on which to get it, once this was everything,
the hard-wired directive, male penetrating female,
female enveloping male, mimicking reproduction,
practicing multiplication, speaking the universal
truth, fuck me, plow me, worship dick, panties
tangled, tampon flung round table leg, animal
linearity, whipping bodies, thrusting, widening muscle,
pubic hair mashed by tidal push, the good stuff,
everything to young, preoccupied, possessed,
birthright blather, now fifty years later grotesque,
tree trunk erection between flabby legs, mush-
room cap, big misshapen oddity with dribbling
slit and withered seed-sack cotton-swaddled,
pulling it out gray-haired crotch, like a retired
cantor, pile driver saddle-saggy, and her orifice
underneath torso, upside-down, dragging
earth, stretched, exhausted, flaccid, jaded of
responsibility, sixty-five year old wisps, this
sequestered exhausted thing mashed in jammies
to a flattened crust, embarrassed and alienated
from itself, like a moldy basement cardboard

box, and who needs it anyway, this is a love
poem nonetheless, how heaviness, illness,
mortality transform erotic compulsion with
ghostly breath, how ashes and the indomitable
spirit still sip the potent potion in their mansions
of blurriness, ethereality, and bewilderment.

*T*WO DAUBERS, we sting each other, our features swell,
you burrow eye-pouch blurring my vision, baking powder
blotches, I stab your lip on Crane's Beach, assassin
sequestered in driftwood hollow, like biplane, I ascend,
bury, transformed to kamikaze—your nemesis—you
knock me, house painting, off ladder to jagged gravel,
tears of agony, eternal red blisters, blinded, blinding,
blunt sore disfigurement transmuted from mud wasp
to lumpy knurl curled in bed like thumb-sucking tot,
I welt, you blister, torturing each, incessantly scratch-
ing, relieving intense radiating fire, tenacity of the
thing, injecting you with me in sacrifice to queen—my
progenitor—I died as did you jabbing needle, falling
away in epileptic quiver, windowpane-buzzing, my
eye puff, two warriors sloughing husks to loftiness,
sometimes obsessive with plastic scratcher I rake my
bites or imagine lopping them off with pocket knife,
bleeding and scabbing, primordially satisfied, you,
too, night's horrific hours, fingers locked into wrought
iron talon tear for joy your perpetual pustules, shriek-
ing with manic, perverse, unendurable pleasure.

*S*HE RECEIVES another lover, he plows her, she opens thighs,
they fornicate in clandestine places, philosophically different
like divergent postulations, testicles bang buttocks, after-
noon, morning, "doctor appointment," she announced,
"client powwow," he informed, interpenetrate, lock together,
reproductive odors, pelvic bone tango, he shoves deep in
cleft, little difference between genitalia, shaft undergirds
both, her erection buried, his external, both stiff, she
who vowed faithfulness sucks his urgent sticky member,
heavenly, dizzying, performed on bed or floor or both
within protective cover, he vibrates like a struck cymbal,
thick girth, the hotter they fuck the more raked my gut,
raw as burn slashed by sirocco, she digs nails into ass to
pull him deeper and I conjure theory of natural selection,
city disgorges few secrets, insulation muffles sexual
groans, above the roof an indifferent moon, they smoke
marijuana to intensify pleasure, smeared perception
increases thrill, strange rooms, new approval, novel
moves, carnality is all, clitoris, penis, friction, possession,
addiction to rushed dopamine, risk, naughtiness, panties
and hair, straps and nipples, zippers and package, cool
fingers wrapping swollen shaft, who wouldn't destroy
a mate for this momentary oblivion and devastation.

I SPLIT FROM myself, abandon myself composing in chair
incomparable verse, float downstairs, sit beside you
on sofa, upstairs achieving immortality I punch plastic
alphabet, swaddled like a neonate in amniotic cape,
upstairs Ajax wrapped in wool muffler, hot-fingered,
composing monument, downstairs ridiculous appar-
ition molded by pillows, breathing, skull with egg-
beaters plunged in brain, sitting on thumbs, I mutter
mother, rhododendron, Luvox, silk pie, snow plow,
concrete abutment, and scald tongue on pekoe
tea, downstairs midget of fleecy slippers, upstairs
voltage Zeus executing people, and arsonist, throw-
ing conflagrations, Melbourne, Mogadishu, San
Luis Obispo, laughing demonically at blistered
people, upstairs plutocrat, totalitarian, fuehrer, father
confessor, I Superman, hammer keys, X, Z, G, braise
corpses into twisted smoking wrought-iron sculptures,
a six foot high tumescent member flaming the
universe, downstairs simper, leg pain, fatigue,
creaking knees, napkins, kisses, chocolate chai
with 1%, fearing corporeal morbidity, the dog
stinks, stroking back of your speckled hand and,
whipped by demons, staring abstractedly, drift
through kitchen for a constipation plum, walnut
pieces, fantasizing matricide, dear oh dear,
upstairs Ludwig Von Beethoven, bristle-tusked,
wild-haired, cleaving flesh of parallel universe like
tender slab of pig, eating my own regenerative
ribs and digits for fuel and inspiration, torque and
acceleration, blood lust and power, downstairs
love's bled cutlet, accident, catastrophe, carpet
cat-hair, lap, mashed coccyx, frailty of attachment
and the smelting cauldron of abandonment, the
white hot needle of extinction approaches the eye.

*I*N A PERVERTED climate I marry myself who is already
married, now I have two partners, myself and she
who share my body, to one I am considerate, to
the other cruel, one I nourish while the other force
feed and berate with shame, one caress, the other
abuse, if I would die for A, I would murder B
whose existence disgusts and whose reflection
embarrasses, yet compelled to betroth myself as
"match made by Zeus," happy bigamist, three in
bed or concert hall, fingers interlaced with one,
arm draped over other, a *ménage a trois* at La
Traviata, I castigate the one intertwined in my
system, digesting my food and excreting my
waste, usurping my brain who entered me intra-
uterine like gravel in concrete, and with intimate
knowledge judged me incomplete, whom I
cannot extract like an overlain net nor kill with
antibiotics, tenacious mate over whom I fume
while ingesting his meat, I have beat him to
bruises, while for she whose face I stroke,
into whose heart I gaze, whose lymph recycles
not my waste or whose chewed lip transmits
pain, I break-dance to Buckwheat Zydeco, lick
like my baby colt, and blow ten grand at the
French Grand Prix of Endurance and Efficiency,
in pink Chemise Lacoste and Chuck Taylor
shoes while sipping Crème de Menthe, other
mate jealously sickens and self-berates after
stuffing down rum cake or engaging in self-de-
rision after committing artistic waste, see this
one, furious and egotistic, shaving my face in
angry swaths shouting worship me, adore
me, catechize and possess me, head in his
head-lock, exclusively and completely, or die.

I FALL IN love with myself and pursue an intimate relationship, I
anticipate breathy midnight confession, getting into pants,
twisting jockeys off ankles into bed trough, French kissing,
burying fingers in flesh, groaning, I'll go down filling mouth
with stiffness, hazel eyes gazing up, salivate to explore
labyrinthine intellect, fathomless compassion, my lead-
walled humility, I approach seductively—Asian Fusion,
Shakespeare in Love, exotic chocolate—fantasize serving
myself champagne strawberries, losing sleep—as once,
previously, smitten by vixen, watching reruns all night
sleepless with passion, striving for distraction, concealing
fetish I steal glances at my feet, privately admire my
prawn-popper fingers, improbable partner, I am by turns
introverted, gregarious, misanthropic, welcoming, stingy,
extravagant, I introduce to elicit thrill and to further
my seduction delicious frivolities: Ouija tiles, Tarot Cards,
The Enneagram, art house movies reinforcing my un-
flagging interest, yet warily I resist the sweet surrender
having suffered earlier the ache of rejection rendering
myself hard to snare, I am not a candy dispenser, my
heart rare as the blood-red lake, but love myself equally
with thick red love, ball of fleshy dense blood-spun
heft, warm and pulsing, and I continue pitching, "love
me, love me, love me," I my own lumbering teddy
with shaggy tum, massive pads, cuddly nap, be, I beg,
companion, husband, fellow dancer, I the dependable,
your immovable rock, tenacious protector—knock
me down, slit me apart, pull back flesh, lay bare heart,
stomach, bowels—steaming compaction—brain, muscle,
organ, nerve—my glistening tissue—body's exquisite
perishable material, evidence of eminent eligibility.

*O*PENING REMARKS, prosecutor accuses of punishable crimes, I do not recognize miscreant, breaking and entering, assault and battery, rape, psychopath with history of domestic violence, narcotics trafficking, armed robbery, her mouth fires bullets, "repeat offender," "menace," "remorseless," "irremediable," "flight risk, "fullest extent," she demands the book, absolute retribution, passion inflames, un-equivocal, "that man before you," "misogynist," "monster," "modus operandi," I squirm, shift, strive for subliminal jury seduction with boyish face, Gary Cooper, Mickey Rooney, innocence unquestionable, testimony complete: psychiatrist, gynecologist, forensic specialist, eye wit-nesses, former wives, officers of law, my reticent public defender wags an impotent redirecting digit, powder blue, shadow pinstripe, prosecutor concludes, "shameless recidivist," rests, plaintiff my love, sweetheart, baby cakes, weariness eats her blood, creases face, sadness laced with malice as she lashes me with fire of seventy tongues: liar, adulterer, abuser, thief, murderer, bully, monomaniac, fake, and I exuding a disingenuous stink, as if I were not the exemplary compassionate helpmate and humanist, heaven sent, her champion, she glares like the silent assassin, sweet pink champagne revenge, swallows anticipatory victory spit, finally wonderful to pave clean slate with brush of boiling tar, even the score, jury files in, "we have, your honor," note like an hors d'oeuvre tray foreman to bailiff to judge, nothing to say, shackled and led away to mind's uninhabitable penitentiary.

*T*HOSE DAYS, crazy days, screaming adjustment, two humans in suffocating cube penetration-intimate berating with bitterness, acid venom, then sex in dysfunctional flat, ice-coffin Boston, piss-yellow backyard floes, crows and disgruntlement of the over-educated Arlington, Somerville, Cambridge yolk-heads, ubiquitous as chicken eggs, and middle-age we routinized, dogmatic, protected ongoing gastrointestinal, psychological, and dental issues, inflexible, making go of marriage, me for the fourth time, cat and dog hair covered, ill-fitting clothes wadded, rage's voltage taser-gun zapping, shouting, roaring, slammed abandonments, bathed in vengeful deep-dug humping, love's Janus shadow of double occupancy, set up of dresser-drawer, dining table, book case, scored heirloom table, floor-scraping camp trunk like Brunswick pins, life's gleaming triangle: insecurity, defensiveness, OCD, man-woman prejudice, I'll be damned, punishing step-children, conditioned emotional mis-interpretation-lashing, slam, crack, pins clatter, scraped clean, me fuming in Rockport motel, you home half-fetal, adults of the crazy days before adjustment, I slugged bruises into my thigh gutturally groaning, mistake, insane, idiot, lunatic, destroyed against your rocketing noise-wall, apartments aren't designed for adult human horror, mercenary biceps, long reach arms, heart pounding militancy, malevolence and malefaction, and cradle-smashing sex, crazy days, psycho days of eternity-destined lovers, cleaved and clung together

formatively ill-fitted, ground however into a
material rainbow-slick ball-and-socket number,
frictionless, coordinated, easefully working.

*Y*OU LOVE me be because I am unstable, defensive, insecure, explosive, I am hair-trigger sensitivity and reflex-retaliation—rage or silent treatment—love biceps and neck veins, battlefield mentality, love my tormenting psychological demons, like Mariana Trench denizens gnawing me original, you love my literary vulgarity, visceral grotesquerie—disembowelments, necromancy—masturbation legions, thin-skinned seething, seed-malignancy wrapped in grape-flesh cellophane, you love the contradictory grinding of compassion and acid, tiresome predictable rancorous unhappiness, you love our horizontal genital gymnastic, my up-curved groin-locked circumference filling you up like poured molten nickel, my rough attention to inches and half-inches, my depth-intellect peopled by suicides, addicts, misfits, wimps, love my snobbery and condemnation of idiots, love my body dysmorphic disorder, girlishness about figures, waistlines, and fat, my checking compulsion and rejection of my parents' infernal longevity, love my abstemiousness dry-drunk dictatorialism and hypocritical fastidiousness, imperfect perfectionism tilting the floor, love my narcissism, comical megalomania, and preoccupation with immortality, love, too, my atheism, avoidance of sanctuaries, oval-mouthed choristers, and theatrical gray-haired organists, love my cornmeal apple-jacks and seafood burritos, my kitchen scrappiness and left-over virtuosity, lovable, too, due to aggressive arrivals up staircase to you, metaphorical or literal pounder of things, voice like collapsing stadium rafters, you my honey bunch, sweetie pie, baby cake loving the great male stamp and hot iron press of me in a world of diminishment, cruelty, sadness, and suffocation.

*T*HIS IS for me, whatever pleasure you get shall be supplemental,
I'm knuckle, stubble, and drive, guiltless, hawk-prey, shove onto
floor, yank up skirt, peeking slash, finish what's begun, closed-
door mash-up, exemplar of what's behind every façade: chill,
cringe, struggle, fear, I'm hauling upstairs to frilly room, raw
flesh against avocado sheets, flaky pie, Pillsbury, Crisco, lightly
brushed, anorectic slut, I know you give it indiscriminately,
striving through starvation for infantilism, appealing to pederasts,
every man wants his child, you are mine, stiff up-curved horn
in muscle-pie, there! haul over you on bed's edge, fascist,
master, god, there, there, and shove in your mouth, however
I wish it, and whatever pleasure you derive is parenthetical,
epithet, powerful little hit, augmented, contrived: painted,
bejeweled, coiffed, starved, dragging scents like a gong, slat-
ternly and cruel, well here's punishment, my masturbation
doll, jerk off rag I shoot magma into, liquid squigglers one
of which might hit, latch, and become, I care not how I
leave you: barren, bruised, conceived, proud, I leave you
gaping, asphyxiating fish on rock, and return whenever
I wish with my swollen shaft, your destroyer, your warrior
in greatcoat, you're meat on whose plate I leave specks,
stay emaciated, remain fantastical with your sticky hips
and bony mound for my next arrival, and next, and my life-
long succession of focused uncompromising appearances.

I WORSHIP YOU says A, I worship you says B, blood pumps
through one heart, one body, two heads, five legs
from a single womb, vault-shut, bonded love, in-
divisible love, heads turn on Siamese neck, kiss, two
throats satisfy single gut, tandem-elimination, gro-
tesque, yes, but what union isn't, while Phillip and
Peg fuck in non-commitment, two instruments fear-
enveloped, he withdraws dangling member flooded
by emptiness gaping her open like a disastrous cut,
both tormented and devious, lonely Hillary cruises
bars, Carmine crumpled by torturous world pushes
himself outward, "seek," "seek," "slay," "achieve,"
while our monolithic creature all revulsion and
beatitude, depleted, sleeps the sleep of the glorious.

PART IV

Not with a bang but a . . .

I **CONFESS TO** insecurity

I confess to hypersensitivity

I confess to defensiveness

I confess to generalized invective

I confess to hypergraphia

I confess to megalomania

I confess to inexplicable misogyny

I confess to totalitarianism

I confess to elitism and snobbery

I confess to criticality

I confess to masochism

I confess to impaling frogs to earth on arrow shafts

I confess to atheism

I confess to frying lizards on spark plugs

I confess to suffocating cats

I confess to homophobia

I confess to fellating Milton, Philip, David, Jimmy

I confess to drunken date rape

I confess adolescent prudery

I confess to four abortions

I confess selfishness and egomania

I confess to extreme onanism

I confess to female psychological abuse

I confess to stiff-necked ideologies

I confess to obsessive-compulsive disorder

I confess to cupidity

I confess self-hatred

I confess to perfectionism

I confess to anorexia nervosa

I confess to rushing myself at mirrors screaming murderous accusations

I confess to swallowed Jewish-fuelled anti-Semitism

I confess sexual preoccupation

I confess to rage at mortality

I confess to personal exceptionalism

I confess classical narcissism

I confess to welcoming others' misfortune

I confess to wishing my father would die

I confess to contradictory interior exuberance

I confess to undetectable pantheistic universal love

I confess to disintegration-vulnerability

I confess to childlike emotional fragility

I confess to refusal to admit dependency

I confess soul-annihilating tenderness

I confess to fascination-with-existence-suffering

I confess unsurpassable infallible intuition

I confess to embarrassment by my conventionality

I confess to a trespassing tactility

I confess universal bewilderment

I confess gluttony

I confess foot fetishism

I confess alcoholism

I confess intolerance

I confess that mother paraded naked before me, pray-peed to me, approached
and withdrew pendulous-breasted like a naughty love-shrew, flashed
thick black pubic bush white tissue-paper flecked, curtains pulled into
bull's eye focus, raced fingertips across penis-head, mock-murdered
with imaginary meat cleaver ridiculous dad, my unceasing worshipful
psychopathic porn star, I at red naugahyde cinema chair, catapulting
this over-sexualized erotically world-laminating man-predator in
which semen sheets down green irises, woman equals incalculable vic-
tories, food fuels muscular buttocks, tongue delivers seductive unction,
touch prepackages licentious oils, Earth is a massive pleasure-pod
squeezed by pulsing hot petal-walls

I confess pumping—drunk, nauseated, desperate—scrotum-strings into ugly
Gail Vandervoort who desiring sincerity and tenderness adored this
monstrous university bastard

I confess attempting to kiss the fat Matamoros prostitute who popped my besot-
ted boy cherry, emptied emission into cum bucket, smoked a Winston
through vagina lips
I confess black-outs, last calls, dead driving, emptiness
I confess romanticism, Camelot, canoes, corsages
I confess to Tourette's Syndrome, impulsivity, disingenuousness, squeezed
obedience
I confess moral ambiguity, screaming downtown, uptown, mid-town, off walls,
down highways, into party barns, beach pavilions, beer joints, apart-
ment houses, drunk, high, sober, stoned, stiff, dizzy, fagged, sick, in
rags, sport coat, Madras shorts, hand-sewn vamps, button downs,
tucked, disheveled, frazzled, slicked-back, ravenous, fat, suave, reek-
ing, trendy, brilliant, feminine, mesmerizing, irresistible, disgusting,
combustible, charming for the piece of ass, the holy Jesus mother-of-
god much demanded piece of ass, some pussy, the good stuff, nookie,
the nasty, action, the roll in the hay
I confess to self-indulgent melancholy whereby I receive compassionate minis-
trations from those with unlimited capacities to give wrenching them
dry and finally, upon revelation, resentful and inaccessible, used up,
furious at their gullibility and my bottomlessness, my sucker-punch of
boyish handsomeness and pliers death-grip, usually care-giver women
sexually addicted to me who go "all in" on eternal happiness, singing
early, struggling later, weeping last, though once an adoring fastidious
man in woven night cap who harbored hopes of homoerotic love and
life-raft happiness at the Alhambra Apartments in Madison, Wisconsin,
but was dashed alongside the female husks wind-blown into concrete
alleyways, and that, too, is love
I confess to reverse Oedipal tragedy, that is, to fantasizing murdering son for
wife's exclusive love for him, her infernal incestuous cooing, coddling,
thrilling his luminous flesh, massages, envelopments, praises, their
insulated-ness, her blunt seductions, shelving me like Yeats's obsolete
doll, when she stroked his cheeks I felt hand's absence on mine, grew
wild, inflamed, pathological, wanted to kill, but killed myself in psy-

che ward florescence, then the marriage, finally him who re-created
mother in crack needle lust and male prostitution, and that, too, is love
I confess under-whelming guilt and the pride to bear it, reptilian leathery
toughness in which blame belongs other-where, on the weak accusing
cowardly victim dragging failure's snail-trail across the world, ex-
cuse-makers for disease and addiction, foam and masochism, "he the
bastard," they scream, "fascistic son-of-a-bitch," sadist," ad infinitum,
using antediluvian soul-wounds to slice himself up in miscalculated
acts of revenge, poor imbecile, flopping filthily in overdose seizures
I confess to etherealism, a disinterested insulting preoccupation with insistent
mysteries, overmastering nonresponsive enslavements removing me
from the millionth millimeter dimensional slit known as "the moment"
into which nothing fits, a vacancy misinterpreted as effrontery, belittle-
ment, superiority, but is instead the freeze of incompetence—what can
this mean, what unmitigated totalitarianism—a gaze neither selfish
nor eliminating but pushed against a lead cerebral wall which by its
impenetrability paradoxically humanizes, and that, too, blast it, is love
I confess to speechlessness which is empathy
I confess to awkwardness which is respect
I confess to anger which is investment
I confess to undifferentiated love which is divine
I confess to envisioning something vague, hazy, red: cherry popsicle, vibrating
light saber, frosted phosphate but alive and curiously human, with-
drawn isotope, strep throat, blood-coursing, vertically inclined, rocket-
ing skyward, enigmatic and indestructible, neon throbbing, swordfish
gill, ruby-warble, tiger slash, oh incomprehensible co-conspirator like
a flitting night disk, sprite or glyph, multifold, sunlight through shut
lids, cat tongue, furry sward, plant sword, inexplicable, radio valentine,
something comforting tall and immovable buried inside and un-dis-
lodge-able, I sleep with it, inner nebulae, dream column, split catharsis,
and that is love
I confess to voyeurism, pornography, debauchery
I confess to sexual nihilism whereby innumerable naked women squirm all over

me licking my entire skin acreage, smearing breasts, giving toenail
polish foot ridge massages, stroking with rough fingers and soft lips,
making me come and come over them, all my rivals lying dead about
me like cricket husks

I confess to blasphemy, and this is love, atheistic laughter, god sardonicism,
Jesus mockery, Papal bobble head and resurrection like thumb-gouged
raspberry jam ectoplasms popped on tongue, I struck Gabriel with a
whipped cream pie, fucked The Blessed Virgin Holy Mother Full of
Grace Mary, jacked off on St. Bernadette of Lourdes' incorruptible
face, stuck a pencil in Father Bartholomew's eye, horrified in surplice,
cincture, and buskins Halloween celebrants, and prayed aloud to fat
gray rat, and let us not deceive, this is plunging reverential erotic
love of the kind that delivers souls from coals, shepherd, staff, lamb,
redeemer

I confess to tremens, Pinocchio shakes, Peter Pan quavers, Cinderella quakes, all
over, ice in brain, ice of deprivation, ice of craving, ice-blanketed like
shocked fever, the quivers and shivers, wrapped in hymen, silk sheet,
broad banner, oh Sweet Melissa, Hot Lanta, Purple Haze, Shiva's
Head Band, Quicksilver Messenger Service, Symphony for the Devil,
Ten Years After, oh, Wind crying Mary, Mary, Mary, oh ships of wood,
Riders on Storms, oh Song of Wind, I get heebee jeebees, frigid rip-
ples, ague fits, sick, the grip, locked in, self-sequestered, imprisoned,
oh fourth bethrothal, Patricia, love, my delicious, oh Southern Man,
Sea of Joy, Can't Find Way Home, let us pray, oh crawling, crawling,
restlessness, hallucinations, depression, fatigue, oh Volunteers, love
thee, adore thee, Pinky Lee Love, Klem Kadiddlehopper love, Who
Killed Roger Rabbit love, Dudley Do Right love, Clint Walker love,
Have Gun Will Travel love, oh Chuck Connors, Sam Houston, Davy
Crockett love

I confess to amateurism and the cult of lost lips

I confess to animalism

I confess to indiscriminate love

I confess to vulgarism covering marshmallow guts

I confess to weepishness, oily rims, packed sugar pectorals, Sherman tank
       constructed of wet confectionary, insubstantiality against fifth estate,
       clacker teeth framed by saggy lobes upon chair-seat cracked red
       plastic snapping air like Pez pit-bull, oozing pyramid of excruciating
       goop, Milky Way, Crème Egg, Mallow Cup, mortality's—like every
       thumb-smudging thing—Bijou-morsel, literally cowardice's nauseat-
       ing lament against non-existence worthy of squirrel carnage and bat-
       tlefield fool, gonads disabused and lifted victorious to unmoved god,
       death before death in a rented tux and gleaming black pumps with
       nothing but Sweet Tart under tongue and a Reese's Pieces dispenser
       head, and this is supreme apical love
I confess maudlin death bed scene wherein mother's interior wasps stung
       unreachable flesh, painful failed-kidney toxin filling helpless inert
       sack, and son's face fallen into birthday cake, butter cream tears and
       green roses snot in hospital corridor at four AM, smeared back of
       hand, abandoned, isolated, mother's oval mouth, son's broken face,
       too late, too late, morphine's claimed the brain and from mother's
       chest son leaps like mouse with cat-teeth tearing rump, what remains:
       an almond-nailed previously-manicured living mass of paste at early
       stage of decomposition, crusted lashes, bag full of waste, son gouging
       with fist from eyes food-dyed pain, a banal bedside death tableau, son
       wearily weeps out into the world
I confess male menstrual cramps, postpartum episodes, mammalian gland-fat,
       broad birthing hips, head-hair profusion, skeletal diminution, high-
       pitched larynx, susceptible to weeps, neurasthenia, hysterics, depres-
       sion, submissiveness my name, woman in magnification, pacifist,
       weakness for whelps kits kittens pups, deferential muscle-mass misfit
       with impact wrench and detester of dictator, vulnerable to rape, spou-
       sal abuse, invisibility, ridicule, invariably overshadowed in a room full
       of guests, irrelevant, insignificant
I confess to object-reverence—idolatry—running lovingly over chair back
       hand, stroking lover's neck of mahogany handrail, walnut desk edge,
       reverence toward and channeling cold tooled granite through finger

whorls, clay, lapis, knotty pine, book's cloth spine and pages-hair,
leather handbag, corn silk, praying awhile, stunned, awestruck, solid
brass sailfish, marble polar bear, silver cutlery, earth-sand, chain,
gold filigree, stiff dog ear, black-to-blue-to-dark amber fur, shocked,
mystified, almost annihilated, heart soft as a third sister, immensi-
ty-diminished, wrenched apart like hot fresh baguette, polished shovel
handle, rich black soil, silence in presence, folded eye glasses, violin,
old slippers, remnants of existence, burlap sack of basmati rice, this
poseur, masquerader slipping out his mail and mace, catching himself
in leg half-buckle tumble to nakedness

I confess to obstinacy

I confess to hubris

I confess impatience

I confess that you are my ocean, butter knife, mountain peak, cartridge ink,
platelet count, PSA, chocolate bacon strip, angel and emanation, my
Winslow Homer, you my chest buttons, model airplane, astronomical
map and every constellation, ladle of cream, sky scratch, fog streak,
dissolving sinking orange lozenge, Australian crawl, sizzling enchila-
da, bible of the primitive and invisible hymnal, you my cartilaginous
mellifluous larynx, you my sky-god, lichen, mushroom, blue corn-
flower, bathtub, leaf rake, you my new roll of Scotch tape, foot sole,
grass and warm concrete, sand dune, triple-blade Gillette and round
bristle toothbrush, I confess to omnipotence in weakness, devotion, re-
spect, sensuality, admiration, you my scallop, pulsing jellyfish, screw
driver, wrench, box of carpenter's syllables and archaeologist's rhyth-
mical notes, my smooth mission glider, my Old Sturbridge Village,
my indispensable pants, my globe circumnavigation back to self, nose
cone, explosion, fire salamander, tongue and epiglottis, you my point
Escondido beach break, my slender-edged lightweight Weber pintail,
my lost frightened iridescent pheasant, my dream utterance, I confess
I am nuts, you my glockenspiel, birdseed and feeder, you my gone
hair and silver Star of David, my Barnum's baked zebra and timing
association, without you I'm Ireland's opposite, you aqualung, bubble

bath, alcohol astringent, spoonbills a-flight, memory catalyst, bitters
spritzer in grapefruit juice, outpointing vector, you my bell buoy At-
lantic-swell rocked, I am paper bull's eye's smoking bullet hole, space
rocket punches through, landslide's suction, you latitude and longi-
tude, my shoe laces, my two half hitches, I am tree pith gnarled round
steel guide wire, you my gorilla glue, my centrifugal point, my fifty
all-time great hamburger recipes, magnifying glass, super hard shell
Turtle Wax, congregation choir, Matisse coffee mug, Ed "Big Daddy"
Roth ratfink decal, country reservoir of meringue cake batter tiramisu
happiness, you my arrowroot teether and topgallant mast, my redeem-
er rock and sneezing tissue, I am duck quack and caterpillar yawn, you
my Earth's magnetic field navigational system, my aurora borealis, my
biological electrical impulse machine, my brain's drawn bow and ce-
dar arrow flying into clock sprockets and rubies and springs, and you
are—dare I utter it, dare I disclose it so jeopardizing is its name—my
honey bunch
I confess to wearing before her invulnerability's self-sufficiency mask, leonine,
alpha, undecipherable, impenetrable, personalities perish against it as
do inanimate architectures, semi-trucks, metropolises, philosophies,
presidential mask, totalitarian mask, I-require-nobody mask, mask of
anguished fragility smashing in others my own cataclysms, impassive
despot concealing dependency on his baby-doll who could summarily
devastate him and without whom he would vaporize, poodle, titmouse,
field hare, child, human disguised as rawhide man, anachronism in
flesh wrapped in pride whose exposure is his worth, without her would
decompose like a freeway mammal spun into ditch covered in beaks,
pincers, enzyme, slime, not indefeasible, I snuggle against her like the
truth
I confess to calamitousness
I confess to accidents
I confess to pornography
I confess to intolerance
I confess to seducing immortality through obsessive-compulsiveness, locking

doors innumerably, turning off gas, voiding already voided bowels,
tightening possessions in mental clamp, wiping guilt with repeti-
tion-rag, squaring, neatening, straightening, lining up, dental flossing
blood flecks before looking glass, and mania, I confess, in the dank
realization I worship myself a god, king pin, pampered cat, this being
love and love's bane and bale and belladonna
I confess my appendages are cavities, ladles, caverns, nets, which holding you,
satiated, fill, feel big as creation, correct, connected, same-requirement
sensual receptors pressed together feel integrated, one blood oxygenat-
ed each two entities, seamless, smooth-molded—touching big—apart
small—big—small—big—small depending on connectivity, like the
incandescent bulb arbitrarily bright or dark through faulty grounding,
so I strive for maximum coverage, mounds filling hollows, curves
concavities, peaks my chasms, dawn blanket doughy warm, such
sensationless ease that rare ectoplasm emanates into the cosmos and
glides among the amplifications
I confess to obsequiousness as when belching "sorry" after McGee shoved me
down a staircase onto playground's hard earthen baldness, notebook
flying, spinelessness as, incredulous and compliant, Jackson's thugs
dragged me unconscious into beach break after pummeling me, who
mounted no defense, insensate, I would have lumbered apologetically
to ghetto to Sobibor to Zyklon bath to belching ash, sure, cowardice,
pacifism, sheepishness, head bowed, thick-sheet slobbering, as when
without recrimination I allowed East Coast ax-man to fling me by tail
like loathsome mouse from my office onto street I should have clapped
the officious smug fucker, this being love, twisted Eros, fat dangling
cow dick in cotton brief swaddle, confess ulcers, cankers, molar-grind-
ing at opposition, sissified predisposition, not-me exposure, acropho-
bic, as when Daddy tummy-mashed me against dining-room bureau
like a happy Nazi sadistically excoriating and I collapsed inside like
empty burlap, all love translating to sycophancy as when Joan promis-
ing sex for Schlitz left me eating street pebbles in a night gutter,
I confess to the cleaned clock syndrome

I confess to holy bloody fucking hell

I confess to peripheries, weirdness, in corners, against walls at prom or game,
disconcerting oddness among contemporaries, tentative heart song, in-
visible computation, freak-o blood drain to invisible, fidgeting fingers,
onlooking, requiring artificial lubrications for am furtively massive,
flexed to scrotum, raw, requiring Mickey's Big Mouth or Swizzle, that
which volts me alive to feel up, to tongue an ear, to peel down, dance
floor dirty toes and black pubic hair, exquisiteness of new love and
flesh wetness netting down legs in crawling sheets, but misfit-ness, not
in game, insignificant

I confess that woman's bare feet constitute total nudity, that sandaled feet
arouse me like naked breasts arouse other men and I am, therefore,
continuously inflamed, French tips destroy me followed my black
lacquer though dance floor filthy also empowers as do chipped and
smeared, strong bony veined ankles tapering to high ridged arches
ditto, stemming from childhood gorgeous Mother's seductive daily
afternoon immodesty in air conditioned bedroom stripped to pant-
ies, fanning toes, painting air with Revlon red, peeing peep show
naked feet balanced on tile, Florida-pink, seductive red mischievous
mouth, stunning to this goddess-struck lad, freckled where it counts,
strawberry pubic mole, toilet paper bits, a roundhouse kick seduction
from she who hating Daddy married son, nail and hammer claw, rivet,
bang, hard dick, delicious, peep show watching sucked out egg yolk
eye, ooh la la, god damn, what a fucking piece, what'd I know, long
steamy thighs, click, click, exposed on brain, telephoto, grained toes
scrimshawed to bone, forehead bone, and that knowing while as we
slaughtered Dad with bladed things, axes, knives, ice picks through
back to vitals, boom dead, and we fucking off to Hollywood, she Rita
Hayworth, Betty Grable, I Van Johnson, William Powell, and how I
took it public gyroscopically—forever, hard yanked chord twisted
round desultorily hanging, I Elizabethan romantic, court lover, Sir
Walter Raleigh, Bacardi-glib, getter-into-pants and unwanted implant-
er, dilation & curettage instrumentation, troubadour pant-waist kneed,

thoroughbred thighs, well, holy banshee cut loose from Mom blowing
blue sand vowels, psychedelic consonants approximating coronets
following a childhood of animal torture, reptilian massacre, and that of
tacks, pins, arrows, fire, winging moths, de-legging hoppers, spear im-
paling, and live sea crabs striking asphalt bouncing forward sixty miles
per hour insouciantly tossed off truck bed like holocaust god, shatter-
ing claws and backs, stalk-eyes bulging, eggs, well, who cares crab
eggs, love this is, negative space love, suction cup-love, affliction-love,
mother's pretty feet, son's fury, mother's scarlet tongue, son's black
lips, mother's racing hands, son's penis-wren, all that taken outward,
Gail Vandervoort, Holly Lanier, Beverly Hudson, Karen Johnson, Sue
Silverman, Catherine Lee Greene, Lea Denmark, sweet sweet Sheila,
the genesis and the truck light experience, innumerable engorgements,
clutches burnt, rods thrown, head gaskets blown, forgotten utilitarian
philosophies, mother blinkered out in my birth hospital and I rolling
about like slapped out eye crying from a socket, I confess brain-lock
stuck-song mania, smoke gets in your eyes smoke gets in your eyes
smoke gets in your eyes, existence-fury popping ropes in reverse,
blinklessness, Mother's cherubic dead oval, sublingual tincture,
de-machined to birth, those surf foam licked olive skinned gams,
coconut oil nape, baking sensuality to this throne pretender, slingshot
arcing outward imperceptible downward curve, Betty Sue, Ginger,
Dominique, sweeps and strophes, love-redemption, love-application,
steering wheel crowds window, horse—blue—engorges pantry, brain
pan be-pedals cinquefoil, spinning I throwing eye water like a cen-
trifuge, oh no! oh fuck! what the hell! on a rust-blood screen, bomb
flash sucking out air cranial ball served hard, ace, mother dead, daddy
nailed abed, love-salvation, love-annunciation, love anti-necrosis, you,
I, immortally mortal without Blue Cross or Kaiser Permanente, pig,
gaping gate, squealing through, high top all stars, green, marines, navy
seals, force multiplier, Nicanor Parra, HD, Henrietta Hawk, free enter-
prise, Patrick Suskind, The Winnipeg Jets, thar she blows! love, love,
air lift, I confess you are my scenic overlook, mist, cathedral shaft,

     laid out mauve quietude beyond the erector set and concrete elbow,

I confess to Barnum's Animals Crackers, Moose Tracks, myoepithelial carcino-
     ma

I confess to sublingual morphine

I confess to sand dabs and finnan haddie

I confess to masculine obstetrics

I confess to Victorinox toothpick

I confess to armor plated rhino

I confess to jangling howdy spurs

I confess to slow deep thrusting atheistic doxology

I confess to raisin bread pudding

I confess to instantiation, atavism, and uxoriousness whatever the fuckinghell
     that means

I confess to Earl of Nottingham, Duchess of York, James M. Cain, Pop 1280

I confess to chocolate lizards

I confess to natal plum thorns and silver chrysalises

I confess to Young Judea summer camp and orthodontics love

I confess to pulchritude and desuetude, word-love, am only angled knees before
     the sanctity of language, each word a god, each god a word, propin-
     quity, niveous, inglenook, susurrus, I pursuer, I contender proffering
     Toblerone, blue delphiniums, irises, coral bells, and diaphanous she
     offering green absinthe and crème de menthe

I confess without you incoherence, pandemonium, mouthful of tongues slapping
     like flags in typhoon howl, cat cries everywhere, sand picked up spun
     into sirocco, pilot pen vulture tattoo on third eyeball, hands cupping
     ears, ancestor, sister, cousin thrice removed, brocaded savior, I bring
     you chrysanthemums, silver balls, lilies of the field, new sharpened
     pencils, inscriber into book of life

I confess to happenstance, accident, serendipity, chance

I confess to double chocolate hot caramel sex over butter pecan ice cream

I confess to stupidity

I confess detestation of sports, men, uniforms, cleats, aggression, pituitary
     emission, turf gnarled toes, hulking irresistible walls head-on clashing

and crumbling through each other, hair swirled buttocks and backs
of shoulders, ego bitten cathartic grunt as seed rushes in, sub-verbal,
Cro-Magnon, XY chromosomal wonders, I disclose certain atrocities
for cleanliness's sake, fantasizing annihilating the testosterone super-
saturated freckle-knuckled class threatening my pharaonic-brilliant
dominance

I confess inhabiting a world of dualities: perfect/worthless, virtuosity/awful,
beautiful/hideous, Gordon /not Gordon

I confess to offensive-behavior recidivism, stomping about, hovering, emanating
stern criticism, flaying you, then with sincere immolating contrition
intoning, sorry, take back your skin, glum, moribund, inflexible, ad-
dicted labeler, "insane," "crazy," "nuts," bodily suffocating you with
harsh suspicions of incompetence poisoning the air, well, I confess to
gluttony, too, compulsivity, unwanted continuous intrusive fantasies,
unequivocal commitment to reformation of reflex through psycho-
therapy and aestheticism only to withstand relapse upon backslide, I
confess continuous uncomforting confessions and apologies

I confess tedium of self, self-exhaustion, monotony of personality who would
be someone else but for fundamental psycho-physiology forcing me
to imperceptible picayune evolutions such as dropping the nervous
giggle or tiny internal prostrations, insignificant impotent adjustments
to the screaming railed machine

I confess to—within flesh-folds, concavities, bones, blood, brain—clandestine
burning religiousness and the need to disguise it with vulgarity, to
plant-reverence, animal-reverence, humankind-reverence, universal
brotherly sisterly love, deity-love, love of digits, ear shells, wrist veins,
ball joints, pelvic clasps, taper and fat, frog-love, water-love, love of
pencil makers and squeezers of paste, lens grinders, spot welders, val-
etudinarians, dunce-flunkies, murderers, butterfly herders, love cat sa-
dists and adulterous husbands, intubated jawless decomposers, failed
portrait artists, and cloud busters, all, all, corrupt avaricious captain of
human souls, he who walks behind elephants, the haberdashery Pope,
roustabout playboy and vicious pugilist, pious leaking softie disguised

as infidel, boiled leather, swell, walking marveler who cannot admit
perishability

I confess envying—occasionally—thick block concrete, its impassivity, insensi-
bility, its deadness and inanimation, how it receives hot darkening rain
and sleet on its skinless bulk, hardens to a nerveless density, unvaried
and null, its object-ness, to feel is to risk, to cry is to endanger, to love
is to expose, I envy what grinds down the chute and thuds into molds
to dry blind, untasting, indifferent, I am unshelled, gluey, wet inside,
lashed by love, intensified, I love so greatly it borders on murder,
one's lover is one's heroin whose shortage enslaves, dependency-lad-
en and skin-stripped stinging, purple and raw, by god, envying—oc-
casionally—poured concrete, immovable, massive, jagged-edged,
near-eternal comfortable in swamp, furnace, ocean, forest, grave

I confess wrath toward everything, greed for everything, ambitionless sloth,
blinding pride, lust beyond endurance, gravitational envy, grotesque
gluttony, add vainglory to that, an eight sin soup thickened with pig
fat, legumes, corn mush and mortared onto skin like a thick lead suit,
I walk in sin like robot man, stiff legged, unbent, irresistible, through
penitentiaries, masonry walls, nuclear reactors, bank vaults

I confess sleeping with stuffed moose, nappy, eyeless, mouth unstitched, dispir-
ited

I confess jealousy of baby-to-mother intimacy, baby need, baby dominate, baby
cling, baby control, baby nakedly stroked, demoting husband to butler,
baby draining kisses and shoving backward rival, baby eating, baby
inter-splicing nerves into nerves, angry male baby sucking her raw,
wanting to slaughter such monster, little pulsing fists, indifferent eyes,
and I launderer, slave fantasizing evisceration, baby helplessness, baby
gloat, and I shot it into her, fathered my assassin, my cruel supplanter
who beguiles the wife, pulls her down into its ruinous bed, husband
devastated, husband enraged, husband impotent, husband destroyed

I confess that I have praised innumerably to myself her body and here is what I
have said: small bones, ring finger size three point five to my thirteen,
slivered almond wrists, thumbs like fingers, foot arches bony bridges

and narrow toes chopped off strait across save for the big inwardly an-
gled ones, all tips translucently pink, frame strung together balsa wood
kite sticks, five foot six, pelvis two empty soup bowls over which
stretched trampoline skin, pale blue throughout skein of veins, visible
interiors into the sub-cutaneous like peeled green grape to its dark
seeds, anterior axial plane hilly, pointed nose, hollows, edges, lakes,
grotto, posterior axial plane gentle foothill slopes, long slides, lifts
and dips, dimples, shivers, sand dune textures, ridges, ripples, sides
bilaterally symmetrical cello in-curves, ears-jawline-chin rosefinch
made human, in another language a small multi-animal mixed-media
being bouncing like water over a secret creek, and such an animal in
her individual parts: fine textured gray-blonde hair swishing about a
well-framed cranium within which works a wicked mind, hair like
corn silk banged and feathered across delicate forehead, temples like
babies wrists cradling in their flesh deep-socketed rake-blade lashed
copper-flecked blue empathies, strong swept brows crowning high
ridges, sharp fin-like narrow-nostril nose upturned in air to allow
lips fully to receive passionately devouring lips, high pointed cheeks
slanting to a kite shaped chin underneath which shallow criss-cross
crinkles, late middle, post-menopausal, sixty winter seasoned, tight
circumferential neck filled with the usual tubing kissed in center back
with a hairline paintbrush tip, unpadded back almost submissive in its
rib-curved boniness sweeping round to modest Pluto-areola teats on
either side and below the xylophone lightly sagging toward an earth
which will one day receive her, baby's crown protruding through birth
canal naval, tummy tent skin stretched over pelvic sticks wrapping
to back-small puckered round a center groove funneled to an upside
down I Love Lucy heart ass, hemispheres split by flat prehistoric
tail wrapping inward to lipped ellipsis, genitals, mound, mons, hair,
happiness expertly packed like a surgical theater or whisper jet cockpit,
thighs-knees-calves wide at hips—cream cheese icing—sliding over
knobs and chutes to skin-wrapped whistles which blow a tweet of two
miniscule six-A sharp balls bridges and pads, collectively a soft starry-

skinned easy-seen intelligent pleasure-perfect naked Caucasian female
    homo sapiens presence

I confess Achilles heels like sheets stretched over cable bridges, her

I confess knuckles like half submerged pistachios, her

I confess fingernails like dimes raining down caught on fingers, her

I confess tips of ears like tips of internal cabbage leaves, her

I confess breastplate like rawhide sawfish saw, her

I confess backs of knees like tiny night-meteor craters, her

I confess rows of teeth like succulent rows of white corn kernels, her

I confess breast cleavage like neighboring eggs in an open carton, her

I confess dark veins of the wrist like a skein of blue wool pressed underneath
    where skin becomes glass, her

I confess ankle pulse like the beloved father's sprinkled reassuring sugar, her

I confess eye cuticle like the liquid rim of a blue Wurlitzer playing Duke of Earl,
    her

I confess hip dimples like phantom pre-historical sexual tail lights, her

I confess shoulder wings like captive's snapped leather harness, her

I confess anus like whirled and twisted fleshy pink cotton candy, her

I confess bear heaviness needs to smash under chest possessively all this, me

I confess stubbornness in which evidence—intuitive, scientific, circumstantial,
    anecdotal—shoots glue balls into my throat, "it is not," "definitely no,"
    "impossible," larynx stops

I confess sadist daddy smoked me to the butt, crushed me out on concrete wall
    with his Nazi anti-Jewish law, verboten at cost of death, rigid back-
    bone, no Butch wax flip, shaved neck, scrub off shit, loathe thyself,
    isolated face, bug host, zero illness empathy, refuse thy passion, no
    hot shot such that rage thermometer blows top at non-provocation,
    slightest lip, even tentative affection, this being also love

I confess soul and corporeal insatiability, infinite hole, shovel till one runs out
    self, then shovel, then despair, I eliminate, incessantly eat potatoes,
    love, pie wedge, bliss, gulper fish, angler, predator love in drug rehab

I confess god aspiration and the frozen hubris peak, planting phallus pole atop
    a Kilimanjaro of slain rivals there to spear Father like a cold mackerel,

love my Mercurochrome

I confess I love your throbbing neck, your tail, your woman-submissiveness,
    taking my large broad cock completely down throat, hands wrapping,
    subjugated on knees below, breasts swinging, toes floor-splayed, your
    not-maleness, how you crave this, flip and hike high ass for rear thrust-
    ing gazing back hair to one side, string of drool and gliding in deep
    groan, then compulsively more sucking stringing spit while rubbing
    spread thigh self, leg over sofa back, then putting me back in slapping
    balls to cheeks ramming back and forth with pure animal playfulness,
    Isadora Duncan arms waving to lesser demons and gods, I love to
    fuck you, I love to fuck you, you offer anus should I prefer, "look at
    you," you involuntarily exclaim referring to my flesh in you, "look at
    you," I flatten you like male barnyard turkey, spread-winged, slaying
    while resurrection-zinging, pummeling and purifying, so much is sex,
    neck-breaking deliverance, spit, spin, bleed, fix, push, fling, slap, lick,
    you fuck-mate, nihilist, feather-dragger, spacewalker, I draw saber
    across your throat, sword swallower, fucking you clothed in church,
    see-sawing before weeping crucifix, prayerful deliverance, mine,
    yours, his, afternoon sun's shafts slicing space like Houdini's chained
    box, bang! we emerge, birthed

I confess to rigmarole, megillah, dyspepsia, fandango

I confess irritability

I confess prodigious appetite preferring melted cheese, stubby toes

I confess biliousness

I confess I detest shoe cleat activities, aggressive males chewing turf with
    polyurethane, leather, steel, wood, bladed or mud blunt, Diatoro,
    Lotto, Umbro, Under Armour, spikes, studs, teats, crampons, dirt
    streaked bodies, grunting, gritting, sacrificial contusion, loyalty, long
    black rawhide tongues folded over, laced back round creak-straining
    bulked oxen muscling, rote trampling down chalk lined fields hail or
    glow, mud rivers, kidney brain knee padded against smashing impact,
    Adonis hung large scrotum youth, cash registered with champion-
    ships, species saviors, glimmered across globe, cleated pimpled shoes

dangling over glory, fragrant uppers, little league, major league, pony
league, professional, fresh jersey pregame crisp crashing through pa-
per posters of ruthless ravens and hard jawed redskins, this detestation
love—romantic love, erotic love, murderous love—this loathing of
cleat-undergirded gorgeous creatures afire with radiance, Promethean
delectations, marrows and meats, the writhing lubricious pitcher's
mound celebrations, eel-like intermixed, producing naked red throats
and gleaming teeth, cleats blinding eternity

I confess the no co-pay, non-deductible intimacy policy offered by God and sold
to cats, weasels, gophers, larks, man

I confess the critical mirror, self-consciousness, nail-in-eye night window, mis-
shapen, corpulent, lipless, parboiled, the accidental glimpse in an oth-
erwise absolute avoidance, lightless baths, shirted sex, one need not
ever espy one's incompetent failed undisciplined self-stuffed through
one's neck known as I, I refuse to dance save alone with myself to rad-
ical music, arms waving, butt swinging, uninhibited, almost dead with
grieving exuberance, you love this clattering dishabille, XXX-large
blanketing shirt, saggy pants, shame as unobtrusiveness, self-neutrali-
ty, what does she love? this female breasted, accident-prone, subdom-
inant, Biedermann and the Firebugs, hypersensitive male who crawls
into a seashell at the heart of which awaits Hewlett-Packard and
private cosmologies

I confess I hosed cold spring water through entrails and am cocaine clean,
water-lathed, impurities slammed away, processing scarlet gills, glass
shard sharp, passion ready, stand-up desirable, liquid oxygen clear,
nitrogen blooming, sheer purity, for you for you for you

I confess emerald and white crystal frog paperweight love; rust-and-light-green
glazed pottery dual-mouth jug love; sterling silver, heavy-weight,
lobster-clasped Judah Maccabee Star of David neck-chain love; box
of twelve-count, number 2-soft, hexagonal, orange, sharpened Oriole
pencil love; glue stick, Scotch tape, black dry-eraser love; auburn-
haired female, blue-latex-gloved, TSA armed security guard frisking
twill-suited stocking-footed male traveler, left hand shoving chest,

right hand stroking wrist, knee lifted between his, lips-touching-lips love; zero-point-one-one oz. orange-blue Gorilla glue tube, Wilkes-Barre Data Operations Center five-by-nine-point-five inch Social Security Administration envelope, one-point-seven-five inch diameter magnifying glass, red CVS pharmacy plastic extra-care card, 40 four-and-one-eighth by nine-and-one-half inch white security envelopes, generic miniature plastic-covered spectacle tool kit, 1954 Fox Fall Focus red spiral-coiled photograph album-ette harboring pictures of birthday boy with new red Huffy, deceased maternal grandparents in early forties, raw slab of family house under construction, boy with big rubber ball love; Barnum's calcium fortified, yellow-and-red Animal Crackers box with cloth white carrying string love; flat-rate ripped-open United States Postal Service mailing envelope curled inside dark burnished copper tin, cheap stamped embossed abstract design, stapled together office trash can love; six-sided line-drawing formed into a box fitted with door, two double-hung windows enclosing one man, like outside-time-space Nowhere Man hunched in squealing slider over black Compaq composing into Dell heart-driven plastic alphabet songs (through rarely using Z) observed by burly brown-and-cream stuffed moose scrunched into cubby, antlers bent over, and pointillist-drawn black tuxedo over white-bodied clay Aptenodytes Patagonicus (King Penguin) adorned with wire eye-hooked-at-knees legs dangling over desk edge love; *World's Fair, Wise Blood, Dead Souls, The Promise, Nazi Germany and the Jews, Rembrandt's Hat, Invisible Cities, Confession of a Mask, The Dybbuk, Pioneer Valley Yellowbook love; Admitting the Holocaust* love; *The Drowned and the Saved* love; *The Death of Virgil* love

I confess to the happiness of perfectly cooked and peeled soft-boiled eggs quivering on buttered rosemary toast

I confess to swinging righteousness to suicide at a starling burst, pacifism to rage at a cat hiss, gregariousness to misanthropy at a pie slice, eroticism to parched leaf at a black syllable, lion to gold fish at a slammed door, pacifist to pugilist at a rail splinter, Olympian to sweetmeats at

150

a water splash, confrontationist to capitulator at a blown fuse, mono-
theist to atheist at a salad burp, virtuoso to crucifix at a tailpipe cloud,
illusionist to rhinoceros in a lip snap, master stapler to gaping ster-
num at a bug bite, insurrectionist to petit bourgeoisie at a lost dime,
animadversions-caster to antimacassar at a touched mole, semiotician
to sledge hammer at a jiggled brow, licentiousness to loquaciousness
at a spigot drop, bibliophile to desuetude at a glass flash, peripatetic to
wedged nail at a rabbi's rites, glissader to glossolalia at a razor slice,
immortelle to Imodium at a blurred shrimp, impressionist to infanti-
cide at a leaf quiver, anthracite to vanilla pudding at a torn door
I confess to Donkey Kong, which is love
I confess to ice smoke, which is love
I confess to bent key, which is love
I confess to pubic hair, which is love
I confess to moray eel, which is love
I confess to blue lichen, which is love
I confess to Bill Hickok, which is love
I confess to mallo cups, which is love
I confess to gladiolus, which is love
I confess to alveoli, which is love
I confess to stuck tongue, which is love
I confess to patricide, which is love
I confess to Scotch tape, which love
I confess to frog dissection, which is love
I confess to Butch wax, which is love
I confess to bearberries, which is love
I confess to terror, which is love
I confess to econometrics, which is love
I confess to pine cones, which is love
I confess to nausea, which is love
I confess to black marlin, which is love
I confess to misdial, which is love
I confess to Coppertone, which is love

I confess to aileron, which is love

I confess to Charles Atlas, which is love

I confess to Bugs Bunny, which is love

I confess to crampons, which is love

I confess to mayonnaise, which is love

I confess to patricide, which is love

I confess to lemon tears, which is love

I confess to Super Sport, which is love

I confess to circuitry, which is love

I confess to caracal, which is love

I confess to egomania, which is love

I confess to petty thievery, which is love

I confess to Revlon, which is love

I confess to onomatopoeia , which is love

I confess to nighttime urination, which is love

I confess to green cabbage, which is love

I confess to narcissism, which is love

I confess to obscenity, which is love

I confess to dead cats, which is love

I confess to sodomy, which is love

I confess to roller derby, which is love

I confess to electric fence, which is love

I confess to bone shard, which is love

I confess to empanada, which is love

I confess to cyanide, which is love

I confess to bicycle, which is love

I confess to hypergraphia, which is love

I confess to inoculation, which is love

I confess to death mask, which is love

I confess to fraudulence, which is love

I confess to humorlessness, which is love

I confess to silver surfer, which is love

I confess to crab louis, which is love

I confess to Vassar Miller, which is love
I confess to Pistol Pete, which is love
I confess to litho top, which is love
I confess to pencil sharpener, which is love
I confess to Camp Karankawa, which is love
I confess to Treblinka, which is love
I confess to Turf Builder, which is love
I confess to archdiocese, which is love
I confess to dog biscuits, which is love
I confess to Rubenesque, which is love
I confess to dead sparrow, which is love
I confess to windowpane, which is love
I confess to sachet, which is love
I confess to imbroglio, which is love
I confess to pancakes, which is love
I confess to theoretical physics, which is love
I confess to Pez, which is love
I confess to cremation, which is love
I confess to dissolution, which is love
I confess to abrogation, which is love
I confess to multiple sclerosis, which is love
I confess to strip tease, which is love
I confess to Christicide, which is love
I confess to anthropomorphism , which is love
I confess to dementia, which is love
I confess to mushrooms, which is love
I confess to green ape gloves, which is love
I confess to archery, which is love
I confess to delirium, which is love
I confess to flocked spruce, which is love
I confess to embodiment, which is love
I confess to apricot, which is love
I confess to torn wings, which is love

I confess to callousness, which is love
I confess to incrementalism, which is love
I confess to absolutism, which is love
I confess to, and that is
I confess to, and that is
I confess to, and that is
I confess to fescue, and that is
I confess to ectoplasm, and that is
I confess to caliper, and that is
I confess to gangrene, and that is
I confess to engorge, and that is
I confess to obstinacy, and that is
I confess to calibrate, and that is
I confess that death nibbles he
I confess that death nibbles she
I confess that death nibbles it
I confess that death nibbles we
I confess that death nibbles they
I confess that death nibbles us
which is love
which is love
which is love
which is love
which is love
which is love
I confess to pesticides, which is love
I confess to anesthesiology, which is love
I confess to fragility, which is love
I confess to chain saws, which is love
I confess to cloud busting, which is love
I confess to acidity, which is love
I confess to intractability, which is love
I confess to lead masks, which is love

da camp town ladies sing this song, do-da, do-da
da camp town race track's two miles long
oh, de-doo-da day

I confess to joyfulness, which is love
I confess to crab-wise, which is love
I confess to plastic fletching, which is love
I confess to silver swell plates, which is love
I confess to bare-breasted figurehead, which is love
I confess to wormy agave tequila, which is love

baa baa black sheep have you any wool
yes sir, yes sir, three bags full

I confess to stringency, which is love
I confess to kibble, which is love
I confess to spiritualism, which is love
I confess to Chevra Kadisha, which is love
I confess to rapid decomposition, which is love
I confess to purification, which is love
I confess to clothes rending, which is love
I confess to anaerobics, which is love
I confess to failure, which is love
I confess to obsessive-compulsive disorder, which is love
I confess to shamanism, which is love

one for the master and one for the dame
and one for the little boy who cries down the lane

I confess to amnesty, which is love
I confess to armory, which is love
I confess to tenderness, which is love

I confess to desperation, which is love
I confess to choleric, which is love
I confess to transitoriness, which is love
I confess to marginality, which is love
I confess to interstellar admonition, which is love
I confess to covetousness, corpulence, intubation, thoracic imaging, scrollwork
         boots, lasciviousness, exegesis, osprey eggs, sleigh bells, colonoscopy,
         bee sting cake, otolaryngology, blasphemy, illimitability, obsession,
         the categorical, troth

famous trumpet man from out Chicago way
number came up
boogie-woogie bugle boy company B
a-toot, a-toot, a diddle-ee-ada-toot

I confess I love her, which is love
I confess I love her, which is love
I confess I love her, which is love
I confess poetry is for the dead, which is love
I confess poetry is written by the dead, which is love
I confess I am dead, which is love
I confess that what follows, verbatim, are her words more honestly and beau-
         tifully expressed than the language of poetry, such as this, which is
         egotistical, presumptuous, and self-aggrandizing:

I love the way I look. I love my deep-set, penetrating, blue eyes—eyes that don't
lie—eyes that penetrate surfaces. I love the etched and swollen skin below my
eyes for the sorrows and joys that have accumulated there.

"I love my body—my small and still-round breasts, my pert and rounded butt, my
wide hips and strong thighs, my delicate feet. I love my aging childlike hands
and tiny fingers, brittle nails and the way the veins crisscross my skeletal hands.
I love my slim ankles, aligned toes and broad feet.

I love my ever-curious and open mind—the way it leads me from one thing to another with a constant sense of wonder and an urgent need to know or understand as best I can.

"I love my sweetness and the way I care and hurt for others.

"I love my mothering and the way I take heart in the accomplishments of my children mainly for their sake. I love the way I have given them their lives and autonomy and that I am now reclaiming my own. I love the way my children can bank on my support and know I will always stand by them regardless of what they do. I love that I am an utterly devoted mother but do not define myself by my children.

"I love that as a wife I have learned to compromise and give the benefit of the doubt to my husband. I love that I am still working on being a better friend to him.

" I love that I can and do spend many hours immersing myself in the natural world around me and that at base I am a beachcomber, birdwatcher, woods walker and mushroom hunter.

" I love that I am modest, somewhat quiet, and that I have no need to puff myself up, or draw attention to myself or to my marginal accomplishments. I love that I do not rely on external rewards and recognition to feel good about myself. I love that it's obvious to me that the world will go on just fine without me when I die. I love that I have no need to "make my mark" or strive for immortality of any kind. I love that I am not afraid of death and can see it as a reasonable alternative to a miserable life.

" And I love that I am no more or no less perfect than anyone else. I love the freedom that knowledge gives me."

I confess awe-inspiration, which is love

I confess stupidity, which is love

I confess this is why I love her, which is love

I confess the end of pomposity, mongrelization, obduracy, arrogance, which is
       love

I confess life enclosed by longitudes and latitudes, which is love

I confess sub-domination, which is love

I confess experience, which is love

I confess inadequacy, which is love

I confess incomprehension, which is love

I confess totality, which is love

I confess miscreancy, which is love

I confess delusion, the delusional, the deluded, which is love

I confess instigation, which is love

I confess tidal pool, which is love

I confess fertilization, supercharged engines, estuaries, which is love

I confess nullification, which is love

I confess non compos mentis, which is love

I confess simplicity, guilelessness, insecticide, which is love

I confess astrophysics and dirty toes, which is love

I confess clairvoyance, paper slice, which is love

I confess idiocy, moronity, prostration, which is love

I confess thesaurus, amphitheater, obscurantism, which is love

I confess antithesis, Diablo, banshee, which is love

I confess cold eyehole, gaping saddle bone, gumless molars, evaporated tongue,
       powdered phalanges, dotted line penis, which is love

I confess preternatural, which is love

I confess licentiousness, lasciviousness, hard candy, Auschwitz, which is love

I confess ignominiousness, gun blast, rectal cleavage, which is love

I confess nothing, nothing at all, women folded in half inside-out in suicide posi-
       tions broken on the boneless lips of God

I confess

I confess

I confess

I confess

this is not the way the world ends

this is not the way the world ends

this is not the way the world ends

(it ended that way for one)

not with a miscarriage

but a verdict,

Preposterous to describe love devoid of metaphor, as psychophysiological
    response, neurobiological reflex, adrenalin, dopamine, endorphins,
    oxytocin, thickening, engorging, purpling, pounding, neurotrans-
    mitters this or that, vaginal lubrication, muscle contraction, blood
    swelling, posterior of the pituitary, palpitations, blush, preposterous
    removing imagery from the language, addressing eccrine and apocrine,
    acid mantle, corpus cavernosum and venous blood, vasocongestion of
    vaginal wall, pupil dilation, bulbs of the vestibule

I have a muse and her name is Patricia

I have a muse who dances the Watusi

I have a muse who feeds me poetry

I have a muse new saddle redolent

I have muse sheds upon bed menopause's Fall multi-ochred leaves

I have a muse with canon barrel eyes stuffed with cornflowers

I have muse bone marrow and monarchs

I have a muse releases from pot lid Shabbat's peppers, tomato, Worcestershire
    steam cloud

I have a muse strokes cats electrical

I have a muse palm-cools forehead, like Xena: Warrior Princess

I have a muse crosses Icarus at Venus

I have a muse with hips everywhere, like a cubist

I have a muse who, under rake-like lashes, reticently pushes, cream-and-lamb-
    bashful, with flesh against my flesh, twisting, knotting, the flashing of
    her passion

I have a muse wearing tall galoshes splashing in my blood

I have muse in rocks and cotton

I have muse peeling off my lip balm, black jackbooted

I have a muse who flays my nipples, knitting skin into rat-hats

I have a muse stiffens to ceiling, toes crashing plaster

I have a muse mellifluous, healing

I have a muse with seven tongues, three-three-one stitched to epiglottis, war-
        bling images

I have a muse ephemeral as a whisker and ethereal as a slough who breathes
        upon my scrotum Joni Mitchell pixies and Chapin Carpenter hues

I have a muse flocked in Old Bodini, New Times Roman, Gaudy Stout, Antigua,
        soles ink-stained, lobes ink-coated, shoulder blades backed into pots
        of spine adhesive, panties deckled pages, phlegm black-thread riddled

I have a muse screams her sexual machinery like a manic-depressive though
        synechdoche

I have a muse with butter-coated mushroom hands feeding me her spongiform

I have a muse cnidarian-diaphanous breast-stroking through death's blood
        like a sticky wedge, filtering through scalloped robe vanity, egotism,
        vainglory, godliness, excretions of mortality-fear like a wacked piñata,
        sloping sweetly through bioluminescence

I have a muse fertilizer-furred, barrow and shovel, hydrangea bush ecstasy, gar-
        den hose, sips diet Pepsi, ice-swirled, after giving it the horticulturist's
        pack down prayer, song of songs, gong, bell, chime, psalm, vibrations
        chasing each other through the new-scrawled air

I have a muse plays cello of beach stones, harp of clay vessels, piano of sheep's
        wool, ocarina of ocean surf, flute of wild mushrooms, hurdy-gurdy of
        driftwood, mandolin of sun vaults, balalaika of gladiolas, yeast bread
        of bare feet, apricot of warm throat, fig cilia/guava hairs/kiwi veins
        of tranquil lake, porpoise-seal-cormorant-blue heron-kingfisher-os-
        prey-piping plover-great egret of the private raw-green and blue open
        space rhapsody

I have a muse smoking menopause

I have a muse glissades chutes, scampers ladders, impacts genetic 5s, 3s, "as
        I see it yes," "my reply is no," "concentrate and ask again," gobbles

160

gum drops, ice cream sea, double purple, licorice stick, prefers plastic
    alphabet tiles, triviality, specialist-tweezed without tripping scream
    from black cavity and permanently repaired bestowing upon it child
    breath, child touch broken forlorn right-cracked heart, "most definite-
    ly"
I have a muse-ventriloquist self-conversing by cabinet and grate, bureau and
    jet with her throat's progenitor, defending, rationalizing, praising, en-
    couraging, schedule of eventsyou can't tell me, I'm going anyway, of
    course I care, I can't believe it, oh look at that
I have a muse—how preposterous to describe devoid of metaphor—rows like
    Sexton's Awful Rower, through bruise-green sky, roiling, wind-torn,
    rain-streaked, collar blown back like silver spear point, planets swirled
    black, stars needle-tight incriminations, moon her denizen-devourer,
    Sextons Awful Rower, lashed alone sodden boat, toward not It, toward
    her sufferers, her mother, her mortality, her gray accepting clay
I have a muse gaggles school children round her like a well, wishing their be-
    longing, transport, wonder, stomach glue, with heart hearth and gather
    she delivers and delivers
I have a muse night cotyledon against winter backed into me under blankets,
    cold moonlight
I have a muse

I have a

I have

I

She like me chin, she like me eyes, she like me shoulders, she like me wrists,
    she like me veins, she like me fascia, she like me muscle, she like
    me happiness, she like me lurching, she like me sweetness, she like
    me confusion, she like me generosity, she like me sinful, she like me
    ravenous, she like me falcon, she like me devastated, she like me
    terror stricken, she like me animadversion, she like me avatar, she like
    me applesauce, she like me stumblebum, she like me marionette, she
    like me tenacious, she like me insurrectionist, she like me bunched
    bundle, she like me ecstasy, she like me insatiable, she like me

recondite, she like me decipherable, she like me petrified, she like me
friable, she like me monotonous, she like me multi-utility knife, she
like me night sky astonishment, she like me iconographer, she like me
dissident, she like me ridiculous, she like me incorrigible, she like me
irrelevant, she like me illimitable, she like me gargantuan, she like me
apricot, she like me prestidigitator, she like me internecine, she like
me zoological, she like me impractical, she like me ethereal, she like
me lymphatic, she like me small intestine, she like me stomach bag,
she like me calcification, she like me salinity, she like me genitalia,
she like me pulmonic, she like me urine, she like me fecal matter, she
like me salivation, she like me mucus, she like me itchy patch, she like
me entropy, she like me bilirubin, she like me hydro-engorged, she
pillages me, she blesses me, she breathes me, she redeems me, she ex-
coriates me, she catechizes me, she crucifies me, she purifies me, she
expectorates me, she exonerates me, she elevates me, she worships me,
she teases me, she washes me, she condemns me, she terrifies me, she
tattoos me, she entertains me, she devours me, she inculcates me, she
humiliates me, she touches me, she possesses me, she infuriates me,
she delivers me, she canonizes me, she transfigures me, she disobeys
me, she kisses me, she chastises me, she babies me, she defends me,
she suffers me, she nurses me, she medicates me, she tolerates me, she
reproduces me, she swallows me, she depletes me, she interrogates
me, she liberates me, she feeds me, she induces me, she hypothesizes
me, she expiates me, she penetrates me, she excommunicates me, she
entreats me, she cross-fertilizes me, she praises me, she bumps me, she
tolerates me, she medicates me, she clarifies me, she psychologizes me,
she resuscitates me, she remodels me, she pummels me, she contra-
indicates me, she silences me, she invalidates me, she alchemizes me,
she electrocutes me, she abbreviates me, she flocks me, she impreg-
nates me, she palpates me, she aspirates me, she etherizes me, she
zings me, she ice-creams me, she indulges me, she balances me, she
unhinges me, she alliterates me, she lances me, she apricots me, she
revolutionizes me, she earthquakes me, she affirms me, she polishes

me, bibliophile, needle worker, clairvoyant, omnibus, she initializes,
as she does, as she will, as she must the unlocking numerical sequence
of the risk, the devotion, and the human flood.

*E*PILOGUE: PERSONALITY predetermines fate: 1. blowhard, delusional self-absorbed, crow-braggadocio blows wife to Pleiades, to Perdition, in dainty paisley tie, mother of pearl links, Pashmina suit, kiltie shoes, tastefully thumping chest reinforcing ridiculousness, fifteen year marginalization of mate who crystalizes in revulsion, derision, and flame-brilliance, and retains in ruthlessness an aggressive divorce attorney to nail to wall his superficial balls, worthless goddamn bastard with his razor cut and pedicure, leaves him sitting on his whisper-jet toilet, constipated and stunned, 2. narcissist, mouth-smearing mirror like midnight slug, shoe-buffed teeth, projecting self in others, gold chemise Lacoste shirt, sun-bronze, hair recon-struction, eating worm-like apple from inside, wriggling out wife's eye or nostril nauseating her, in brain, heart, stomach, soul thousands of him oblivious in part and whole to his corruption, hollowing her but preserving skin for pretty lampshade, blown-out egg shell, heedless and unknowing and making love to a spiritually decimated limp love-starved windsock, 3. trollop, strumpet, slut, whore combining in her flesh-laboratory spermatozoa of four sweat-ecstatic men—husband, workman, lawyer, friend—minor indiscretion—she could swallow four more, four again, insatiable, voracious, addicted of course, husband beat her fur-iously—she liked it—but obsequious, he, nonetheless, Proust scholar, peed on his precious Ph.D. in postmodernism and French literature, imitating Burroughs, gin sloshed, fired a pistol at her but missed and sadistically indifferent disappeared down alleyways chased by laughter's suicidal echoes, no passion ensued, just a clinical embittered unfulfilling fuck, 4. Peter Pan, Puer Aeternus, Sky King Bat Masterson Bill Cody, forever roping, flying, riding, racing, sports enthusiast, Double Bubble, light flash flit, our boy in Havana with espionage toy, wife, femme fatal, prostitute, mistress, volleys against the underlying radio-logical horror, discards Jacks, Queens, hold twos, threes, places no bets, runrunrun, danger lurks behind eyelids, tag you're it,

Simon says, mother may I, freeze, don't move, go but fast, alone
forever with Milton Bradley, Revell, Matel, Ed "Big Daddy" Roth,
and endless Wendy until, creased antediluvian unrecognizable
to self, gray asphyxiation in a locked garage, 5. hypochondriac,
physician-pantheist, gynecologist of the reproductive psalms,
oncologist of Deuteronomy, urologist of the Apocalypse,
medicine cabinet chock with unction, here lies the primary
relationship, fidelity, admiration, dependability, trust, validation
by sympathy, serum, powder, tincture, tab, wax suppository,
zinc milk mixture, lovemaking to amber plastic vial, obsession
with sleep mask, surgeon of salve, child's nurse-maid, friend-
psycho-therapist, wife-administrator, all whirling about
tumor like a Red Cross truck, pork chop red skin asparagus
server, cocktail straw floating atop iced lime rickey, in-
dispensable but nonexistent, invaluable but mashed paper
thin by centrifugal force, house a sanitarium and all the rooms
themed for cure: white for sterility, cerulean for peace,
green for regularity, red for release, 6. nihilist whose cross-
word puzzle gapes for "angst," "Rasputin," "anomie," "post-
modernity," "nothingness," "emptiness," "self-destruction,"
"libertinism," "Frederich Nietzsche," "Leopold von Sacher-
Masoch," "Bataille," "Pier Pasolini," "hedonism," "futility,"
"depravity," "addiction," "Godlessness," "fatigue," love is
futility, obedience dumb, politics immaterial, religion ob-
scene, everybody screws everybody drunk, high, hallucinating,
scarified, Caligula-nauseated, emotionless, bellyaches, urine,
groans, cheek-slap reports in the great orgy halls of moral
and ontological nihilists, lustfully murderous, indifferent, sex
partners snapping like chain reaction mouse traps, soak
brain with liquid grain, sardonicism, boisterousness, expunge
sin of monotony, the human life-rag, eyes awhirl like pin-
wheels scorching the dull white air rubicund with deadly
thrill, who cares, what difference, who gives a bloody shit,

7. liar-thief, whose co-inhabitant cannot find the floor, the
edges, her own incisor teeth as she drops through world's
bottomless crease unspooling fingerprints like flesh-colored
thread, where am I? what seam is this yawning to magma
core? Mariana Trench? Post-Millennium Trough, hands
invisibly fast, where's shelf, root, rope, what does one
catch when catching untruth? she drifts to Advocate Lutheran
Hospital psychiatric ward while lair-thief with jeweler's
ball pein waltzes through museum, boutique, patisserie,
street breaking with his tiny pate plate glass, display case,
clock-face, vase, and 8. all the rest: intimidator, passivist,
pleaser, passive-aggressor, megalomaniac, materialist,
perfectionist, masochist, paranoid schizophrenic, idealist,
romantic, hedonist, mediator, rationalist, humanist, messiah,
martyr, authoritarian philanderer, sentimentalist, creator,
evangelist, healer, dogmatist locked each by animator and
possessor in the gorgeous vault of the overestimated self.

Acknowledgments

Descant (Canada)

CV2 (Canada)

Drunken Boat

Court Green

Columbia Poetry Review

The New York Quarterly Foundation, Inc.

New York, New York

Poetry Magazine

Since 1969

Edgy, fresh, groundbreaking, eclectic—voices from all walks of life.

Definitely NOT your mama's poetry magazine!

The *New York Quarterly* has been defining the term contemporary American poetry since its first craft interview with W. H. Auden.

Interviews • Essays • and of course, lots of poems.

www.nyq.org

No contest! That's correct, NYQ Books are NO CONTEST to other small presses because we do not support ourselves through contests. Our books are carefully selected by invitation only, so you know that NYQ Books are produced with the same editorial integrity as the magazine that has brought you the most eclectic contemporary American poetry since 1969.

Books

www.nyq.org

poetry at the edge™

www.ingramcontent.com/pod-product-compliance
Lightning Source LLC
Chambersburg PA
CBHW081417090426
42738CB00017B/3398